# Just an Orange

## CLARE LEVY

**Authentic**
LIFESTYLE

Copyright © 2003 Clare Levy

Published 2003 by Authentic Media

09  08  07  06  05  04  03    7  6  5  4  3  2  1

Authentic Lifestyle is an imprint of Authentic Media,
PO Box 300, Carlisle, Cumbria CA3 0QS, UK
and PO Box 1047, Waynesboro, GA 30830–2047, USA
www.paternoster-publishing.com

The right of Clare Levy to be
identified as the Author of this Work has been
asserted by her in accordance with
Copyright, Designs and Patents Act 1988

**British Library Cataloguing in Publication Data**
A catalogue record for this book is available from the British Library

ISBN 1–85078–491–4

Quote in Epilogue taken from *1001 Great Stories and Quotes*
By R. Kent Hughes © 1998
Used by permission of Tyndale House Publishers, Inc.
All rights reserved

Typeset by Waverley Typesetters, Galashiels
Cover by Diane Bainbridge
Printed in Great Britain by
Cox & Wyman Ltd, Cardiff Road, Reading

# Contents

| | |
|---|---|
| *Prologue* | vii |
| CHAPTER 1 | 1 |
| CHAPTER 2 | 7 |
| CHAPTER 3 | 15 |
| CHAPTER 4 | 23 |
| CHAPTER 5 | 31 |
| CHAPTER 6 | 39 |
| CHAPTER 7 | 47 |
| CHAPTER 8 | 53 |
| CHAPTER 9 | 58 |
| CHAPTER 10 | 67 |
| CHAPTER 11 | 76 |
| CHAPTER 12 | 82 |
| CHAPTER 13 | 89 |
| CHAPTER 14 | 93 |
| CHAPTER 15 | 96 |
| CHAPTER 16 | 102 |

CHAPTER 17 · · · · · · · · · · 107

CHAPTER 18 · · · · · · · · · · 112

CHAPTER 19 · · · · · · · · · · 117

CHAPTER 20 · · · · · · · · · · 121

CHAPTER 21 · · · · · · · · · · 124

CHAPTER 22 · · · · · · · · · · 130

CHAPTER 23 · · · · · · · · · · 137

CHAPTER 24 · · · · · · · · · · 142

*Epilogue* · · · · · · · · · · 150

*To the man with the*
*'circular tuft of dark hair perched on his mostly*
*balding head'*

*with fond love*

# Prologue

If God has forgiven my sin, if God has called me to be his child, if God really loves me, why is he allowing these things to happen? The painful cries of one little girl, diagnosed with an inoperable brain tumour, echo through the following pages, and with hers other voices start to gather.

How does a Christian mother cope, looking on as her daughter struggles physically and spiritually? How does a Christian father hold a frail family together? How does a teenager cope with paralysis? How can the church help?

When it seems as if this family can take no more, God shows himself to be most present. He does have a grand purpose. As a potter, beating and pummelling clay to create something sublime, he is at work, shaping a life that causes the world to wonder, the angels to peer, and the devil to tremble.

*Names and identities of some of the persons and places in this book have been changed in order to protect people's privacy or prevent embarrassment to them or their families.*

*Emma – a cheeky three year old.*

# Chapter 1

It was winter 1986. The early-morning light was grey and murky. A small bungalow clung precariously to one of the many suburban streets on the southern Welsh hills. Inside, a family was having breakfast, as usual.

Paul, a lean eleven year old, sat spooning cereal into his mouth, eyes barely open. His father, Pete, stared listlessly into his tea. Emma, eight years old, a cheeky little thing with a mass of red hair, was chattering noisily. Liz moved around them all, seeing to breakfast.

Pete sluggishly finished the last drop of tea in his cup. 'I wouldn't mind another one, love?'

Liz glared at him. She would have to make another pot now. He did this to her every morning. If she put two teabags in the pot he would be fine. This morning she had put one in and he wanted another cup. Muttering to herself in the kitchen she heard a clattering noise, then Paul shouting, 'Mum, something's wrong with Dad!'

She looked around. Pete was slumped like a dead man over the table. 'Pete, are you all right?' She got to the table, shook him a little. 'Pete! Are you all right?' There was no response.

She looked up, furiously trying to think. She was a qualified nurse. She ought to know instinctively what to do.

'Paul. Go and call an ambulance.'

She pulled Pete off the chair on to the floor, moving his arms and legs into the recovery position. He was so limp. Kneeling over his face she could feel warmth. He was still breathing. She could hear Paul's faint voice from the other room.

'Are they coming, Paul? What's the matter?'

He appeared at the door. 'They won't believe I'm serious, Mum. They won't believe me.'

'I'll go. You stay here.'

Paul stood over his father's sleeping form, his young mind racing, turbulent.

'Yes, that's right. Peter Freeman. He's forty-one years old. We live at 20 Hill Drive. Yes. He's still unconscious.'

All this time Emma had been screaming. Now she was hysterical, running the length of the room, her face awash with crying. 'My Daddy's dead, my Daddy's dead!'

Liz dialled another number. 'Marilyn. It's Liz. Something's happened to Pete. I need someone here to be with the children. Can you come?'

Marilyn, her twin sister, lived in the next street to them. She would not be long. Liz put the phone down and checked Pete again. He was still breathing. 'Don't cry, Emma. Daddy's going to be all right. He hasn't died. He's going to be all right. Paul, I think you had better ring Aunty Sue as well. Can you do that for me? You're being so brave.'

Blue flashing lights appeared in the window. The ambulance had arrived.

'What have we got here then, Liz?'

The voice was warm, familiar. Two hefty paramedics towered over her – Peter and Moelwyn, close Christian friends. Pete had been best man for one of them. Strange they were on duty today. She felt the first pang of relief since she had seen Pete's slouched body. She stood back, watching them, as if in slow motion.

'He's starting to come round, Liz.'

They moved Pete with professional ease on to a stretcher.

Marilyn and Sue, Pete's sister, had arrived.

'Can you look after the children, Mar?' asked Liz. 'We'll go with the ambulance.'

As the ambulance doors closed she heard Pete at last speaking faintly.

Marilyn looked into the room. The breakfast table was strewn with dishes. The contents of a freshly made pot of tea seeped into the cloth like an ugly brown birth-mark. On the floor, an overturned chair. On the sofa, two shaken children, one silent, one inconsolable.

In hospital Pete suffered further seizures and then curiously, as quickly as they had arisen, they ceased. Tests were inconclusive. He had probably experienced an epileptic fit of some sort, although the doctors were unsure.

'Have you been under any particular stress recently?'

Pete recounted the events of his week – he had helped a friend and his family move to Sweden, a round journey of over a thousand miles. The doctor grunted. His collapse was most likely induced by exhaustion.

'Take things a little easier, will you. You can go home. Take these tablets for the epilepsy and no driving for two years.'

At home they slotted back into their normal routine. But Emma was behaving oddly. She could not forget her father's collapse. It seemed to remain in her consciousness, dominating her every waking moment. They were so used to a noisy daughter filling the house with cheerful prattle. Now she was anxious, tearful, obsessed all the time that Pete would die.

In the mornings she would hang on to his legs as he went through the door.

'Promise me you'll come back, Daddy.'

If he dozed off in his armchair she would crawl all over him.

'Wake up, Daddy, wake up.'

And she began to get headaches. They would come from nowhere.

'It hurts, Mum, it hurts.'

Then they would disappear again. Sometimes she would complain of feeling sick. The episodes seemed innocent, but she was having a lot of them.

One morning Liz confided in her mother-in-law. 'I just don't know what to do. Since Pete had the fit she's just not herself any more. And she seems to have so many headaches. They've been going on for months now.'

She was reassured gently. 'She'll be fine, Liz. It was a shock for her seeing Pete collapse. It's bound to take time for her to get over it. And as for the headaches, you'll be on holiday soon, and she'll be on the beach and in the sea. They'll disappear soon enough. Try not to worry yourself.'

They had booked their holiday to the Isle of Wight a year ago. As July approached they felt in dire need of it. It would be good to get away and put the stress of the year behind them. They were going with Marilyn and her husband, Dyfrig.

They made an early start, packing up the two cars in the hazy light of morning. By the time they pulled up to the docks the day was hot and sticky. Interminable queues coiled ahead of them. Pete switched the engine off and stretched himself out for the wait.

'What's Mar doing, Pete?'

He looked up. Dyfrig was ahead of them in the queue, at the check-in point, and Marilyn was getting out of the car and walking over to them.

'I don't know. What's up, Mar?'

'Oh, Dyfrig said I should join you. He's going in another lane for smaller cars.'

They inched forwards. Dyfrig drove on to the ramp. The horn sounded. The ferry started to sail. Emma started to cry. 'Uncle Dyfrig is going without us!'

Pete was unconcerned. 'No, of course he's not, Emma. They're probably turning the ferry around and they'll load cars on the other side.'

They sat and waited some more. They could make out a figure on the top deck that looked like Dyfrig. He was standing alone, looking poignantly back to the shore. The figure got smaller and smaller until it was just a speck. Liz voiced the unthinkable. 'Pete, I don't think this ferry is turning.'

The sisters started to giggle.

'He hasn't got any money. He doesn't even know the address of the hotel.'

Soon they exploded. They laughed until their sides ached. But in the back of the car Emma was working herself into frenzy. Fat tears streamed down her cheeks.

'We won't see Uncle Dyfrig ever again.'

'Don't be so silly, Emma. Of course we'll see him again.'

'He hasn't even got his "joy riders" with him,' she sobbed, as the adults roared all the more.

Sitting on deck, tasting the salty air, Emma snuggled into her mother.

'I've got another one of those headaches, Mum.'

Liz looked at her red swollen eyes.

'I'm not surprised after the day we've had. Don't worry now, Emma. Let's enjoy this holiday. We're going to have a great time.'

As they drove off the ferry, there Dyfrig was – and smiling. Emma cheered up and within minutes her head-ache disappeared.

After the somewhat eventful start they settled into the long lazy summer days. Every morning they waded through mountainous breakfasts of bacon and eggs before pitching their striped windbreaks on the beach and lying out on gaudy towels. At lunchtime they moved to the quaint Thistle Café to indulge in frothy ice-cream sodas and creamy desserts. Emma would announce daily to the bemused owner, 'We're back!'

But as the holiday progressed she complained of more pain. The headaches seemed indifferent to the island air and sunshine. If anything they seemed to be getting worse. By the end of the week she had to lie still on the beach towel until the pain had passed. With each new headache Liz worried more.

On the return ferry, Liz stood with Mar on the top deck, watching her two sunburnt children race around. Apart from these headaches Emma seemed so healthy. Why did she feel so uneasy about them?

'I am concerned about her, Mar.'

'Why don't you take her for a check-up when you get back? It might be something simple. Perhaps she needs glasses.'

'Yes. I think I'll do that. I could be worrying needlessly.'

# Chapter 2

At home, Liz booked an appointment with their family doctor. She explained that Emma had been having headaches. 'They come on suddenly. She often feels sick with them. They don't last long.'

The doctor listened with a blank expression and went through the usual checks. 'She seems fine, Mrs Freeman. But perhaps you should get her eyesight looked at. She might be overstraining her eyes.'

Liz made an appointment with the optometrists' practice Pete used. The first available was that Saturday morning. She would be working a night shift on Friday but it was important to sort this out quickly. 'Yes, we'll take that one. No, she hasn't had her eyes tested before.'

Saturday came. They sat in the waiting room, flicking through the magazines.

'Emma Freeman, please?'

Emma raced into the room and on to the chair. The willowy optometrist began his examination. Liz sat quietly in the corner; the darkened room was sending her to sleep. She jolted her head, straining to keep her eyes open, when she noticed something. He was going back again and again to Emma's left eye. After what seemed like an age he put his instrument down.

'Would you wait outside for a moment, Emma? I want to talk to your mum about something. The receptionist will look after you.'

Emma skipped out. The door closed. Liz was awake now.

'I believe I can see raised pressure behind Emma's left eye, Mrs Freeman, and I would like my colleague, Mr Jameson, to take a further look. I think we should do this quickly,' he added carefully. 'Would you mind taking a private appointment?'

Liz swallowed before replying, her mouth suddenly dry as dust. 'No, not at all, whatever you think is best.'

With that he picked up the phone and arranged the appointment.


Pete saw something was wrong when they got home. They endured the afternoon, eating supper together before putting the children to bed. It was late when he finally asked Liz what the matter was.

'The optometrist is worried about her eye, Pete. He thinks the pressure behind it is high. He wants her to see an ophthalmic consultant privately.'

'When?'

'He can fit her in on Monday morning – at his home.'

They said very little after that. The television was on, a trivial game show, the screen emitting canned plastic laughter. They suppressed any fears as the weekend crawled on.


On Monday morning they sat nervously in Mr Jameson's tasteful private consulting room. He put Emma in his gargantuan leather chair, drawing the curtains before beginning the hushed examination. It lasted longer this time.

'I'm going to be using an orange dye solution, Emma. This will light up the vessels in the back of your eye for me. Sit quite still, now.'

She winced a little as he inserted drops to dilate her pupils. Liz and Pete could see her scrunched-up face in the darkness. And they could see Mr Jameson going back over and over again to the left pupil, fixing on it with intense concentration.

'Good. I think we're done. You've been very patient, Emma. Would you like to go outside for a moment? I just want to speak to your mum and dad. We won't be long.'

He looked at them both steadily, pausing before beginning.

'I've been able to examine the whole of the back of Emma's eye, Mr and Mrs Freeman. I'm afraid I have to agree with my colleague. The intracranial pressure is high. There is definitely something there. I think now it would be wise if we asked a neurologist to take a look.'

Something there . . . a neurologist . . . The words came out like splintered glass. Reeling, they sat as he rang the consultant's office. 'Yes, yes. I'll tell them.'

'Dr Farrell is not available at the moment,' said Mr Jameson. 'I've asked his secretary to give him my message when he returns. He should be in touch with you very soon.'

He shook their hands kindly as he let them out.

The roads through the city were busy: they had hit the lunchtime traffic. Businessmen were out for lunch; schoolchildren were loitering outside newsagents. Late, they arrived home. Unlocking the door they could hear the telephone. Pete answered it. It was the secretary. Would they take Emma to Dr Farrell's private clinic in the morning?

He drew breath. They wanted to see her that quickly? He looked over at Emma, scattering her coat on the floor as she came in. 'Yes, that'll be fine.'

'Emma,' said Pete, 'another doctor would like to take a look at your eye. We'll go down first thing in the morning.'

'All right, Dad.'

Paul had turned on the television.

'Can I go to Richard's house for the day?'

The two children sprawled on the carpet, eyes glued to the set.

On Tuesday morning, the three of them sat in yet another muted waiting room, Emma chattering happily. As Dr Farrell appeared in the doorway, Liz bit her lip.

His examination lasted seconds.

'I think we'd better have you in for a scan, Emma.'

He turned to Liz and Pete.

'They are expecting her. Just pop her down to the children's ward as soon as you can.'

Liz found the suspense almost suffocating – more doctors, more waiting.

As they walked back to the car Emma was thoughtful. 'Don't you get lots of presents in hospital, Mum?'

'You do – and lots of cards.'

'That's all right then.'

Half an hour later they pulled up in the hospital car park. Liz knew her way around the buildings, reaching the ward instinctively through the maze of tunnels and corridors.

'This is the children's ward, Emma, through these doors.'

A group of nurses stood around the ward desk. One of them looked up as the doors slammed noisily.

'Liz Freeman?'

Liz knew the voice.

'I don't believe it – Ruth Davies. I didn't expect to see you again!'

Years before, Ruth, a highly competent staff nurse, had guided her through her pre-nursing training. So now she was a ward sister.

Ruth looked at the three of them kindly. She had heard that Liz had two children. This must be her daughter. A sprightly child with a doll-like face stared up at her. She was tiny, with striking waist-length red hair.

'What can I do for you, Liz?'

'Dr Farrell sent us. He said you would be expecting us.'

Ruth felt the grin on her face ebb away. An hour ago one of the consultants had briefed her on a new case coming in – a young girl with a space-occupying lesion in her head. This was the little girl – Liz's daughter. How awful. Sensing their unease, she collected herself.

'That's right. He did phone through this morning.'

She looked smilingly at Emma.

'We have to send you for a scan, I believe, Emma. Come with me and we'll see what we can do with you.'

Taking Emma's hand firmly, the wiry sister disappeared. Within minutes, Emma returned in a heavy wheelchair, wearing a shapeless hospital gown.

'She's going straight up. The porter will push her. You can go with her as well, Liz.'

They made polite conversation through the corridors and before long they were in the scanning room. It was pleasant enough. In the middle sat the scanning machine. Emma scrutinised it slowly, the strange white metal box, with a dark hole scooped out of the middle.

The radiographer introduced herself.

'Good morning, Emma. We're going to take a few pictures of your head. It's nothing to be afraid of. You lie

down here and will move slowly through the machine.
You just have to make sure you lie quite still.'

Emma nodded, all the time looking at the hole. In there
– she would be going in there.

Liz stood listening, her mind wandering. She knew a
little about CAT scans; spinning X-ray machines allowing
a computer to take cross-section pictures. She knew they
were looking for a growth of some kind. From the
continued interest in Emma's left eye the growth was
probably there.

She felt Emma tug at her sleeve.

'I'm right here, Emma, right here.'

The radiographer injected a solution in Emma's arm
and helped her on to the slab-like conveyor. Then the noise
started, clanging, vibrating. Emma felt herself inch her
way into the mouth of the machine, as if she were being
swallowed whole.

'You mustn't speak to her, Mrs Freeman. We don't want
her to move at all.'

'Can I sing to her?'

'Well, I suppose you can sing.'

Holding on to Emma's foot, Liz sang Sunday school
songs and hymns they loved, as if they were the only two
people in the room. Half an hour later the noise ceased.
Emma slowly emerged from the machine close to tears
and Liz wrapped her up in her arms.

As they left the room the radiographer shouted after
her: 'Nice voice!'

Ruth met them on their return to the ward.

'Now, Emma, would you like to see the playroom? I
shall introduce you to some of the other children on the
ward. There are quite a few.'

This was more like the hospital stay Emma had
imagined. She was out of the wheelchair in an instant.

Pointing to a small side room, Ruth lowered her voice slightly. 'The doctor will be coming shortly to speak with you both. You can wait in there.'

And so Liz and Pete waited for the pendulous minutes to end. The door opened. They looked up to see a junior doctor enter the room. She was a young woman and she seemed nervous. They knew immediately the news was not good. She gave them a hesitant smile before fumbling through her wad of X-rays and clipping a film on to the light box.

They could see her pointing to something. They heard vague words, faintly, as if in a dream.

'Emma has a tumour. It's about the size of an orange, situated in the middle of her brain, in one of the four ventricles. It has been moving around and blocking the cerebral fluid. That's been the cause of her headaches.'

Pete broke the deep silence.

'What are you going to do about it?'

'For now we will start her on a course of steroids to help reduce the raised pressure.'

That was it?

The junior doctor looked down, her cheeks reddening. 'The consultant will be able to tell you more. I am sorry.' Gathering up her notes and X-rays she left.

They sat in silence staring at the wall, staring at the hollow light box.

'I suppose we had better get back. People should know.'

'Yes. People should know.'

There was a payphone in the corridor. Pete dialled the number for Paul, staying at his friend's house for the day. He could hear the dial tone. What could he say to him? He couldn't bring himself to tell him about the tumour.

'Paul. It's Dad. I'm phoning from the hospital. Emma's being kept in overnight. Mum's going to stay with her.

I'll be down later to take you home. Yes. I'll give her your love.'

Liz found Emma playing happily with the other children.

'Emma. The doctor wants you to stay in hospital tonight. I'll stay with you.'

'OK.'

She barely looked up.

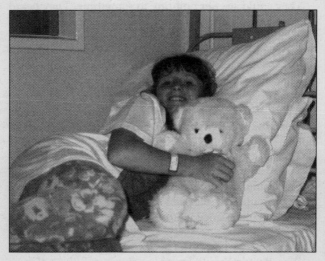

*First days in hospital.*

# Chapter 3

That night Liz took up residence on a makeshift mattress alongside Emma's bed. It wasn't long before Emma dropped off. She was tired after the eventful day.

For Liz, sleep did not come so effortlessly. The ward was full, horrendously noisy. Children were crying. A little boy, suffering from diabetes, screamed each time a nurse attempted to inject him with insulin.

For the first time that day she was alone and her thoughts were riotous. It had all happened so quickly. This time last week they were a normal family. On Saturday she had been a normal mum taking her daughter for an eye test. Today was just another Tuesday, another chunk of time in the daily round. And yet it had brought with it – she couldn't even say the words.

If she was honest she had known that moment in the darkened room; that moment the optometrist had returned to her daughter's left eye with measured intensity. She had known then that it was a tumour. She had known it sitting in the waiting rooms of the various specialists; known it holding Emma's foot in that scanning room; known it when that poor junior doctor came through the door, clutching the wad of scans for dear life.

In the darkness, in the movement of the ward, fragments of the last few days were being relived with an almost tangible agony. In desperation she cried out to God:

'You've just got to help us. Take it away. I don't want it to be there. I want them to say tomorrow that it's gone.'

The night seemed endless, a perpetual agony. The mattress was uncomfortable. No position offered sleep. She turned to one side, then the other. By the early hours she was still awake.

The ward was quiet now. Nurses were outside. Children had drifted off, followed by exhausted parents. Ward lights were dimly lit.

She could determine Emma's sleeping form in the shadows. She loved to watch her children when they slept. She loved to sneak in on them, mouths open, warm flushed cheeks, so wonderfully formed from within her body. She looked beautiful now.

Liz pushed the thin covers off and sat on Emma's bed. She remembered reading in the Bible about elders of the church laying hands on the sick. She had a desperate compulsion to do that for Emma. Maybe God would hear her cry. Gently, she laid her hands on her daughter's head, over the place of the tumour, and prayed for her again.

She heard voices outside the ward. A nurse put her head around the door and closed it again.

Sinking back on to the floor, she fell asleep.

In the morning things were a little brighter. The ward was full of activity: first the medicine round, and then breakfast. Pete arrived with a pile of cheerful cards and they sat exchanging news as Emma tore open the envelopes. It was almost eleven o'clock when Ruth came by the bed. In hushed tones, as if announcing some impending disaster, she told them: 'Mr Beeston is on his rounds. He's coming to meet you shortly.'

'Who's Mr Beeston?' asked Emma.

'God,' Ruth replied.

In a moment, Mr Beeston stood at the foot of her bed, glasses on the edge of his nose, looking quizzically at her chart. Emma stared wide-eyed at the stately figure before Ruth led her away to the playroom. Pete and Liz stood up and shook his hand. He was, apparently, one of the finest neurosurgeons in his field. Brusquely, he motioned for them to sit down. He had little time for small talk.

'As you are aware, Emma has a brain tumour. I'm not sure whether we will be able to operate on it. From the scan it seems the tumour is seated right in the centre of her brain. If we were to try she would face the risk of brain damage, paralysis, blindness. She might even be left unable to speak.'

He stopped for a moment. A young couple stared back at him, hanging on to his every word, and yet every word was damaging them badly. Sensing their hurt, he lightened his tone a little.

'However, her timing is impeccable. A meeting of neurosurgeons will be taking place at our hospital this month. I will present her case to them and we will consider her options together.'

Pete heard more words, faintly, as if in the distance. This couldn't be happening to them. Emma seemed so well – she had a few headaches, that was all. He heard something else.

'Sorry. I'm sorry. Could you repeat that for me?'

'I was saying that I might be able to insert a shunt into her head. This would drain off any excess fluid caused by the swelling. This might work for a time. Are you ready for me to explain things to her?'

Pete nodded slowly, gripping Liz's hand. 'Yes. That would be kind of you.'

'As she's only nine, I don't want to frighten her with medical jargon, or even the word tumour. I suggest we describe the problem as a blockage.'

Emma was summoned to the bed, cheeks hot from running around. She didn't stop to look at her parents. Her eyes were rooted on the consultant. She was completely mesmerised by him.

'Emma, will you sit down for a moment. I want to tell you something. Inside your head you have what we will call a "waterworks" system. This has become blocked. That is why you have been having headaches. I am going to try and unblock it for you. I have a lot of friends who are doctors and we are going to see if you need an operation. In the meantime you will have to stay on the ward and have another scan. Do you have any questions you want to ask me?'

Emma sat, barely listening to his words. All she could think was: 'He doesn't look like God to me!'

As the neurosurgeon departed and Emma returned to her friends the bleak diagnosis finally sank in. They knew now that this was not going to go away. From the fragments of information they were gathering, the road ahead was going to be a long and painful one.

They sat together, Mr Beeston's words beating in their ears. Pete said suddenly, 'We need to tell Paul about the tumour. He's got to feel that he's part of this. From now on he should be the first to know.'

Liz nodded blankly. 'What about anointing Emma with oil, Pete? Perhaps we could ask Mr Fry?' John Fry had been the pastor of their church until recently.

Last night seemed a dream now, that moment of complete aloneness with God, by this very bed.

'Yes, we must do that. I'll telephone him after I've spoken to Paul.'

Before the day was out everyone that needed to know about the tumour knew. The following day, and the next, visitors trickled in and out of the ward with presents and cards. Slowly, their days settled into a consoling routine.

Emma seemed completely untouched by all that was happening. She had thought it was a little odd when her old minister had put some oil on her head and prayed for her, but nothing more than that. Life in hospital was still a bit of a novelty. The days were punctuated with various procedures, which helped to pass the time.

She had seen a child psychologist who had put her through an assortment of intelligence tests. She had excelled in all of them. She had to take a daily dose of steroids. She had lost count of the times a nurse had appeared with a needle to take a sample of blood – she was getting quite used to needles now. The EEG to test her brain function had been the most unpleasant, having to sit still while weird electrodes were placed on her skull. She had another CAT scan and this time it was not so much of an ordeal. The radiographer quite enjoyed her mother's singing.

All the time she felt really well. Her headaches had stopped. She had more energy. She appeared to be back to her old self.

For now, they simply had to wait.

Towards the end of August Mr Beeston came to see them, Ruth close by. He looked cheerful. It had to be good news.

'I am pleased to tell you that we reached a decision in our meeting yesterday. We were unanimous in our opinion that a shunt would be the best option for Emma at this stage. We are concerned about the pressure in her head and don't want to delay the operation. So I will see you, Emma, in the morning. Do you have any questions?'

Emma thought furiously. In three weeks' time she was going to be a flower girl at a friend's wedding. The dress was hanging up in her wardrobe at home – white organza with a pink satin sash. She even had a matching parasol. She had been looking forward to this for ages.

'Will I still be able to be a flower girl?'

'I don't see why not. I only have to remove a small patch of hair from your scalp, my dear.'

He turned, leaving Emma speechless. She couldn't face people with a bald patch on her head, let alone be a flower girl.

Ruth sat down next to her.

'Now, don't you worry. Mr Beeston will only need to take a patch from the back of your head. And your hair is so long it will fall over the bald spot and nobody will notice. He doesn't understand how important these things are to girls. I can ask him to shave the hair when you're sleeping. Would you like me to do that for you?'

Emma nodded. It didn't sound quite as bad when Ruth explained it like that.

In the morning everything seemed set. They were waiting, Emma in a white gown and ankle socks, ready for theatre, when a visitor poked his head around the door.

'It's Uncle Morton!' Emma exclaimed.

Morton was a friend from their old church, Lonlas Mission. He was a dear, whimsical man, glasses teetering on his bony face like full moons. Liz was relieved to see him. He was always absorbing company. He had a delicious sense of humour and donned the most ridiculous outfit at church parties.

He sat down on the bed.

'Hello, you two. A little bird told me you weren't well.'

'She's just going up for an operation this morning, Morton.' Liz dropped her voice. 'They're inserting a shunt into her head.'

His generous face fell.

'Well, let me wait with you, my dears.'

He sat by the bed, amusing them with daft stories and jokes, up to the moment the nurse arrived with the trolley.

'I think this is my stop, Emma. I shall be praying for you.'

With that he left suddenly. They hardly had time to say goodbye. Within minutes Emma was on the trolley and Liz was busy gathering up her things. As she followed her daughter through the unyielding ward doors she turned around for a second and saw him, head in hands, sobbing in the empty corridor.

In the pre-op room the theatre team fussed over Emma. Mr Beeston dropped in, fully masked and gowned, to see her before the operation. Emma flung her arms around him and planted a loud kiss on his cheek. The anaesthetist started to count. By four, Emma was unconscious. Liz left for the ward to wait. By midday Emma was being wheeled back on the trolley.

Days later, as she was convalescing, Mr Beeston paid them another visit. He informed them the operation had gone smoothly and the shunt had been successfully inserted. Why then did they sense some unease in his voice?

He showed them the new scan pictures.

'These have confirmed what I originally thought. Emma's tumour is positioned deep within the brain. It will never be removed.'

Never be removed ... The words swam around Liz's consciousness. That was it: a death sentence. She forced herself back to the consultation.

'The pictures also reveal that the tumour has two parts to it. One part is calcified – in other words, old. The other part is new and growing with its own blood supply. It is highly possible that the tumour is congenital.'

'You mean Emma has had it from birth?'

'Yes. It has probably lain dormant until this year when somehow it started growing again.'

They could not allow themselves to ask the inevitable question. Mr Beeston answered it for them.

'We still do not know if the tumour is cancerous. I didn't attempt a biopsy because of its position. For the time being at least I think we will leave things well alone. Some children seem to survive with a tumour present in the brain. We will check her regularly and wait.'

As he left the ward, he caught sight of his affectionate patient.

'You can go and be a flower girl now, Emma.'

Emma remained in hospital for a week and then was allowed home.

# Chapter 4

In a way things were harder then. The need to go home had been crushing: if they could only take their little girl away from hospital, they had thought, life could be reasonable again. But however hard they tried they could not get the tumour out of their minds. It was continually present, lurking in Emma's brain, growing insidiously, ensuring her life would never be the same.

The first Sunday home they got ready for church in the usual way. They had to try at least to reassemble the familiar patterns of family life. Emma was well – ironically, she was perfectly healthy. The steroids were working wonders. She had lost her sallow look, brought on by months of prolonged headaches. Her cheeks were like little peaches. The scar from the operation was invisible, hidden under her long ponytail.

People were thrilled to see them. They had been praying for them solidly over the last weeks. Emma looked completely well, and Pete and Liz seemed so positive, albeit a little pale. After the service they were swamped, hugged, questioned, all at once.

'What's the latest news, Pete?'

'Well, they've done all they can for now. It's inoperable you see. But we're trusting in God. Who else can we trust in?'

They were so full of faith – it was remarkable.

They said their goodbyes, drove home and came in to
the comforting smell of the Sunday roast crisping nicely
in the oven. It hadn't been so much of an ordeal.

But all was not well beneath the brave front and routine.
Liz began to feel as if the layers of their once-'normal'
lives were being peeled back to expose an agonising mess.
In almost every waking moment she found herself poring
over Emma's childhood to the very earliest days for something she had done wrong. What if she had eaten something when she was pregnant with Emma? What if there
had been some sin in her life that God was now punishing
her for?

Every night she would pray with Pete, something they
had done since the early days of their marriage, but
although the usual words came out, inside she was
beginning to lash out at God. She felt so angry. How could
he have allowed this to happen to her little girl? How
could something good possibly come out of this?

She thought of her friend Philippa, from Lonlas. She
had lost her five-year-old daughter to cancer not so long
ago. She remembered the funeral day, the tiny coffin. She
could see Philippa's face, so brave, her eyes visibly shining
with faith. Philippa had told her that through it all,
through all the suffering, not once had she doubted God.

Not once. And yet here she was. She couldn't see
God's hand any more. The walls, the ceiling, seemed to
be closing in on her. God seemed as distant as the North
Star, twinkling faintly a million miles away.

Some nights she would let her mind roam over the
connecting years of her life, trying urgently to reassure
herself that God had been with her. And if he had been
with her, surely he wouldn't abandon her now.

She dug out her earliest memories. She was one of four
children born into a poor mining family: two boys and

twin girls, herself and Marilyn. She remembered her mother sending them off to Sunday school in Moriah, a crumbling Welsh chapel in the village. Her brothers would stop at the door, make sure their sisters were installed safely, and then steal away to play football in the field.

When they moved to a council house on the other side of the village they changed Sunday schools. This time a rickety bus collected them, dropping them at an apostolic church in a nearby town. The services were in English this time, but still made little impact.

She remembered her mother's stroke. She was thirteen when it happened, the first of many. She had watched her with big eyes, lying in bed, her left side virtually paralysed, wondering how they would manage now. In time the girls realised it was up to them. They left school as soon as they were able and took turns to nurse her and care for the family.

And then there was Geraldine. They had been such good friends. They had worked together when the Addis factory opened in Swansea. She remembered the conversation they had one morning, sitting on the production line.

'Will you come to church with me on Sunday, Liz?'

'It's not my scene, Geraldine.'

'It's not mine either, but I've got to go.'

Geraldine's parents, Tom and Alice Benjamin, were Christians, attending a small mission hut in Skewen.

'I've got nothing to wear.'

'You don't have to wear a hat, you know. Go on. Come with me for moral support.'

That Sunday they had made their way nervously into Lonlas Mission. An hour later they were outside again.

'It wasn't too bad. I suppose I could come with you sometimes.'

That had been the start.

All of a sudden, everywhere she turned, God seemed to be speaking to her. They discovered that one of the managers in the factory was a Christian. He was a thickset man with a circular tuft of dark hair perched on his mostly balding head. Every Monday he would make his way over to the girls as they cringed and whispered to each other: 'Alan's coming. He's going to ask me if I went to church.'

Looking at them through thick-rimmed glasses, he would leave them with the foreboding words: 'I'm praying for you.'

Then Geraldine's mother had died of breast cancer. The funeral had been such an odd service, full of joy somehow. Everywhere people were talking of Alice.

'She's in a better place now.'

'She's gone to glory.'

They were such queer things to be saying at a funeral.

And then there was her mother. The repeated strokes had damaged her body and mind until she was unrecognisable, a mere fleshly shell.

Death and dying seemed to be all around her.

Something was drawing her to the mission hall each week. She kept hearing this Gospel being preached. People were praying for her. She felt her mind opening up to all kinds of possibilities. Perhaps there really was an answer to death. Perhaps there really was something more to life.

One Saturday night in January 1967, at the Sunday school anniversary services, the preacher gave out a stack of 'decision leaflets'. She had taken one home, reading the words repeatedly. Alone in her bedroom she prayed for the first time, asking Jesus to forgive her sins, to give her eternal life. She went downstairs. Her father, the worse for drink already, was sitting by the fire. She decided not to say anything. They were all calling her 'Salvation Annie' as it was.

The next Sunday morning in church she still could not summon the courage to tell anyone what had happened to her. On Sunday afternoon there was a special service at which a missionary couple, Reg and Grace Tomlinson, were speaking. She knew she had to confess her new faith in Christ that afternoon. It was now or never. The moment the service finished she pushed to the front of the hall. People were milling around her. She found Mrs Tomlinson and put a hand on her shoulder. The words spilt out: 'I've asked Jesus to forgive my sins. I think I've become a Christian.'

As she did so, Geraldine appeared by her side, tears pouring down her face: 'I want to decide for Christ too.'

How strange that God had brought them to faith at the same time.

A few years later Grace and Reg were shot down on their doorstep in Canada by a deranged man, martyrs for the Gospel.

Liz shook herself back to the present. She could hear Pete's turgid breath in the room. He had only just dropped off. Sleep did not come so readily now.

She remembered how they had met. The night she had decided for Christ she had been engaged, but her fiancé had not shared her new-found faith. The pastor of the church had shown her Bible verses that seemed to imply she should break off the relationship. She had taken little notice of his words. It was Tom's nagging insistence on the matter that changed her mind. 'Will you do one thing for me, Liz? I promise I won't say one more word on the subject if you go home and read this passage in Corinthians three or four times.'[1]

---

[1] 2 Corinthians 6:14–18.

On the third reading she was convinced. Confiding in a friend from the mission, she was told firmly: 'God will honour you, Liz, in what you're doing for him. He'll give you someone better.'

Unknowingly, she had already met him. That New Year's Eve in the mission hall she had been introduced to a strange-looking man, thin as a pole, wearing a long shabby mackintosh. She hadn't given him a second thought, whereas he had announced to his friend, after taking one look at her thick dark hair and piercing green eyes, 'That's the girl I'm going to marry.' By October they were engaged.

She remembered her sister's horror the first night she took Pete home. Mar had stood in the doorway, slowly taking in the appearance of this figure in a dingy overcoat, before asking him in.

Pete had a somewhat different reaction on taking Liz home. His father had seen scores of girls come through the door, but this one was different. He had heard a voice announce brightly, 'I'm Liz.' Looking up, he had thought to himself, 'There's never going to be another girl coming through this door.'

Pete had a startling testimony. Despite his puny frame, he excelled at sport, especially cricket and football. At seventeen, he was kicking a football around with friends. They were just about to start a match when he felt a sudden overwhelming urge to make his peace with God. Shouting to them, 'Sorry boys, I've got to go and find God,' he ran off into the town to the nearest church he could find and hammered on the door.

The pastor of the London Road Presbyterian Church had just returned from six months' sick leave. He very nearly sent Pete on his way, but something stopped him. He could see the boy was genuinely searching. He invited him in and in one of the musty rooms of the chapel led him to Christ.

At the time Pete was working as an apprentice in a cloth-cutting factory. As he worked, he preached, so much so that the manager eventually had to stop him: 'Please don't do that any more, Pete.' He had been witnessing to one couple in the factory, Charles and Doreen, for some time, but to no effect. One Monday night he was praying for them when he felt God tell him clearly that they would be saved that Saturday. There was a mission on in one of the large city churches and he decided to invite them. On Friday night he called to see them. 'You are coming, now, aren't you? I'll come and pick you up if you like.'

As Pete walked into the church with them he whispered to an usher: 'My friends are going to be saved tonight.' As they took their seats in the gallery, he asked a couple if they would kindly move: 'They're going to go forward tonight to make a decision; you don't want to be in the way.' Before the preacher had even announced his appeal, Charles and Doreen started making their way down to the front of the church. They were saved that night, as God had said.

Liz turned over for what seemed the hundredth time that night. In the darkness, the memories kept sweeping in waves over her, ebbing and flowing, exciting years, painful years. God had been with them both so clearly, so directly. He would be with them now. She had to trust him somehow, with the feeble strength she felt she possessed.

If the tumour had always been there undetected maybe it would carry on like that, present but not felt, controlled by the little tube the consultant had expertly placed in Emma's head.

The wedding Emma had been so anxious about came and went. She wore her candyfloss dress and had her hair curled into masses of tight ringlets. She looked radiant.

The months crept on and by the end of the year she was back in school and coping well – there was nothing to set her apart from any of the other nine year olds in her class. Mr Beeston weaned her off the steroids. Apart from the occasional check-up she was more or less discharged.

Perhaps it had all been a fright over nothing.

*A flower girl after all.*

# Chapter 5

The following spring, Emma's teacher took the class on a field trip to a local nature reserve. She had asked Liz if she would go along as a helper. It was a warm morning, sunlight dappling the vast lake, and the children were enjoying themselves, taking notes and making nature sketches.

Liz looked at Emma. She could see her group intently examining a hollowed tree stump. Emma stood apart from them, awkwardly, her face discoloured.

'What's the matter, Emma?'

Emma looked back. 'I've got a headache, Mum.' She paused. 'I feel sick.'

Liz started. Emma had not had any headaches for nearly a year, since the time of their Isle of Wight holiday. She sat her on one of the park benches.

'Just rest a little, Emma. You'll be fine in a minute.'

They leant together quietly, their minds racing. Toddlers scampered around in the playground behind them, screeching with laughter. Class groups clutching clipboards and pencils meandered to their next task. Liz felt estranged from all around her, the old dread rising again. In ten minutes the pain had eased and Emma rejoined her friends. She scolded herself for her worry. It could have been a normal headache. It was probably nothing.

Days later she sat down with a cup of tea to look at photographs she had just collected from the developers. That March they had celebrated Emma's tenth birthday and a group of friends had come to the house for a party. She skimmed through the pictures, smiling to herself. It had been a good night. One photograph made her stop suddenly: Emma, posing in a new sweatshirt, staring right into the camera. Her eyes, there was something wrong with her eyes.

Liz put the photograph down and cried. How hadn't she noticed before? The pressure had returned. The whites of Emma's eyes were full; her pupils were low, like setting suns.

After a few moments' sitting, waiting, she telephoned Mr Beeston's office.

'Hello, it's Liz Freeman. My daughter, Emma, is under Mr Beeston's care. She has a brain tumour. I think we need to see him again, urgently.'

The secretary remembered them.

'I'm sorry, Mrs Freeman, but Mr Beeston's in theatre all day. I will get a message to him for you as quickly as I can.'

An hour later the telephone rang. He would be able to see Emma at five o'clock in his office.

Emma breezed in from school. She noticed her mother was quieter than usual.

'What's the matter, Mum?'

'Nothing's the matter. I'm in a bit of a rush with tea. Mr Beeston wants to see you in the hospital at five, so we'd better get a move on.'

'Why tonight?' she asked, pinching a raw carrot from the chopping board.

The potatoes were boiling over now; a thick white mess appeared on the cooker top. Liz pretended not to hear as steam hissed through the kitchen.

It was nearly six o'clock by the time they saw Mr Beeston. He examined Emma's eyes, balance and co-ordination, his face set, expressionless. Immediately he sent her for another scan. As soon as they returned he sent them to the hospital pharmacy to collect medication. He was restarting her on the steroids.

Alone with Pete he placed the latest scans on the light box. Pete recalled the first time he had seen these translucent films, the first time he had seen a picture of the orange in his daughter's head.

'It's not good news I'm afraid, Mr Freeman. The tumour has grown and the shunt is obviously not dealing with the excess cerebral fluid. I think she will need another operation.'

He explained carefully and slowly the next procedure Emma would have to undergo. It would involve connecting a piece of tubing to the existing shunt, through her neck and abdomen, into her stomach. Any excess fluid would then drain away instead of building up.

The next morning Emma found herself in theatre again.

This time the waiting was worse. She was upset going into the pre-op room. 'Don't let me go, Mum. I might not wake up. Please, Mum.' Her cries echoed as they sat in yet another hospital waiting room, willing the endless minutes forward. The operation appeared to last longer. Finally, they received word that she was out, and a nurse took Liz along to the recovery room.

Mr Beeston stood upright and dignified in his theatre regalia. He had just looked in to check on her progress. Emma, drowsy from the analgesia, spotted him in the corner. 'Mr Beeston, thank you, thank you. I'm so sorry I was upset before the operation. Please forgive me.' To his astonishment, she sat upright and grabbed him around the neck, smothering him with kisses. The theatre nurses flicked their eyes at each other. No one usually went near the distinguished neurosurgeon! He coughed stiffly and removed himself from the room.

'Do you know, Emma? I'm sure I saw a smile on his face then.'

An hour later, back on the ward, he spoke with Liz and Pete again.

'The catheter is an emergency measure. It has been inserted successfully and will work for the time being. The fact remains, however, that Emma's tumour has grown. Our problem is this. She is still growing and the tumour in all likelihood will grow with her. Puberty might well accelerate its growth. Although we cannot be sure, I have decided to treat it as malignant. I have referred her to Dr Sinclair, a consultant oncologist. He will meet with you in a few days' time, after Emma has had time to recover from surgery.'

With that he departed.

Pete and Liz sat for a moment infusing his words. This time yesterday, Liz had been sitting down with a cup of tea, looking at photographs. Within twenty-four hours, Emma had undergone major surgery, and now she was being referred to a cancer specialist. It was almost unbearable.

After a while, Pete went to make the necessary phone calls. Liz sat near to tears.

'Come on, Liz, you have to be strong for Emma.'

It was Ruth.

'That little girl needs you. You mustn't ever show her you've been crying. Children pick up on all the vibes, you know. Pull yourself together.'

With that the trim strawberry-blonde sister left. Liz felt duly reprimanded. Of course Ruth was right. She washed her face, dried her eyes, and went back to Emma's bed.

A few days after the operation Emma was recovering well and looking forward to a spot of entertainment Ruth had organised for the children on the ward. A clown was staging a show that afternoon. Chairs were laid out in a circle and children gingerly placed in seats. Emma sat in her striped pyjamas, dwarfed in an enormous red-leather armchair. The clown appeared to a round of applause in his baggy suit and spotty bow tie – the children loved him.

Liz stood watching the act from the back of the ward, hiding behind a pillar. She was dragged out and before she knew it was centre stage, wearing a red nose and singing silly songs! Emma looked on proudly. Her mum was a good sport. She always joked around – now she had the nose to match!

They were due to meet with Dr Sinclair the following day. Ruth showed them into the interview room. 'I warn you now, Liz, he will paint a very black picture,' she said. 'So be prepared.'

A wiry-looking man entered the room. He had springy hair and big glasses. He sat down and began straight away. They were used to the remoteness of Mr Beeston, but Dr Sinclair seemed completely abstract and austere. He had a dreadful cold and, in between sneezes, he related the worst news to date.

'Emma's tumour is known as an "ependymona". With this type of tumour minute seeds can be thrown into the cerebral fluid. There is also a danger of the seeds reaching the spinal column. So I have decided to treat both Emma's head and spine with radiotherapy. There are risks involved. The first is that Emma may not reach puberty naturally if damage to the ovaries and pituitary gland occurs. The second is her growth may be stunted. However, Emma is tall for a ten year old, and has a head start.'

The couple listened carefully to the consultant, still not really knowing what he was saying to them. Pete put their fears into words: 'We don't really know what we're up against?'

'In my experience,' replied the oncologist, 'there's a thirty per cent survival rate into the teenage years.' He paused slightly. 'If she makes it to twenty-one she's done very well. The treatment will take place daily over a six-week period. She will have regular blood checks. She will experience vomiting and tiredness. And, of course, as the radiotherapy is mainly on her head, she will lose all her hair.'

Up until this point Liz had been listening, immobile, trying to control her emotions. But this was pitiful, the thought of her daughter losing her beautiful hair. 'All of it?' she whispered. 'It'll all come out?'

Finally the unbearable tears came. Pete sat helplessly as his wife cried. Dr Sinclair carried on sneezing.

'I do need to speak to Emma. Could you bring her in, nurse, please?'

Ruth retrieved Emma from the ward.

'Hello Emma. I'm Dr Sinclair. I'm going to be looking after you for a little while. We're going to be treating you with X-rays. You might feel a little tired and sick, but that will pass. You will also lose your hair.'

'How much hair will I lose?' Emma asked quickly.

'All of it,' he replied with another sneeze.

'You mean I won't have any hair at all? I'll be bald like my father?'

The tears welled up. She had been through a lot, but this was unthinkable – her beautiful hair. As far back as she could remember, when people described her, the first thing they noted was her hair – it was so much a part of her. Nothing to date had been as bad as this: the headaches, the tests, the scans, the operations. Something inside her came apart. She sat in her mother's lap in torment, sobbing, not knowing where the tears were coming from, and not knowing if they would ever stop.

Pete watched his wife and daughter, aware that the decision lay with him. Years ago they had decided, while raising their family, that he would make the final decisions. Now he faced his hardest one to date. He had never been a particularly muscular man, but his strength of character was to sustain the family now. He signed the consent form and went to telephone his son.

Lights were out in the ward. Emma, worn out after Dr Sinclair's visit, was sleeping soundly. Pete had left for the night with Paul. Liz lay in the darkness unable to sleep again. She relived the last few days in her mind.

Unless a miracle happened she knew her daughter would never have a normal life or even a life at all. Emma might only see the difficulties facing her now, but Liz saw all her hopes for her disappearing – school, college, marriage, children. Why had God allowed this to happen to her? Why Emma?

Pete didn't see it that way. In his solid, matter-of-fact way, he was more resolute. Why should God spare them suffering?

The doors to the ward opened and closed with rhythmic monotony. Liz turned over and tried to doze.

'I've come to see Liz, Emma Freeman's mum?'

Liz recognised the voice. A nursing friend had just come off night duty to see them.

'I'll go and have a look now and see if she's awake.'

The day before, the friend had sat on the bed and talked excitedly about her new house, barely asking about Emma. She was a good friend, but . . . Liz moaned quietly: 'Please, Lord, I can't face this now, not tonight.'

When the duty nurse came near the bed Liz snored softly a few times.

'Sorry, they're both fast asleep.'

As the doors closed, Liz prayed to God for forgiveness, and turned over.

# Chapter 6

Emma had only a few remaining days left on the children's ward before she was discharged. She would undergo radiotherapy several weeks later as an outpatient at a neighbouring hospital. Before she left, Ruth attempted to persuade her to try on a few wigs. 'They'll look pretty on you, Emma. Go and try some on.'

The subject of hair was still a sore point, and the thought of a wig was even worse, but Ruth was insistent. 'I know a hair salon that specialises in wigs. You should give them a call, Liz.'

Liz rang from the hospital, explaining briefly about the tumour, the hair loss that would occur, and Emma's nervousness.

'That's no problem. Bring her down. We'll see what we can do.'

It was still spring and an obstinate fine drizzle had descended over Swansea. Emma, feeling frail, was excited at the prospect of a trip outside after the monotony of ward life. Chris, another aunt, collected them from the hospital and drove them into the city.

The salon seemed to be closed. They rang the bell. Nobody answered. They were starting to get wet. Eventually a sour-looking woman appeared and showed them into a storeroom at the back of the building.

It was cold. Boxes of hair solutions and rollers lay scattered around. A few chairs were hurriedly laid out for them. They looked at each other bleakly.

'If you'll just sit there, in front of the mirror,' the woman said roughly.

She pulled out her selection of wigs, all of them heavily set. They would have suited an old lady, maybe, but certainly not a young girl. She pushed and pulled at Emma's scalp, trying various sizes and different colours. Emma sat mortified.

'Have you got anything similar to my hair?' she asked nervously.

'Don't be so silly, child,' she snapped. 'That's impossible.'

Liz, looking in the mirror, saw tears rolling down Emma's cheeks.

'Stop crying, child. It's only a wig.'

That was enough.

'I am sorry,' Liz announced, appalled at the inconsiderate treatment Emma had received, 'but we're leaving now.'

They left the salon, helped Emma into the car, and went straight back to the hospital. At visiting time, Liz confided in Pete: 'It was the nearest I have ever come to thumping anyone!'

Ruth suggested another salon and, hesitatingly this time, they booked an appointment. The owner, David Carlsson, gave them a somewhat different reception.

'Why, hello, you must be Emma. I've been looking forward to meeting you.'

He ushered them into a lounge for coffee and biscuits before getting down to matters in hand.

'Did you know, Emma, you can have a wig made using your own hair? There's a firm in Banbury specialising in the technique. I would cut your hair short now and use the locks for the wig. When you start radiotherapy there will be less of it to fall out. It might be easier to cope with.'

For the first time since the meeting with Dr Sinclair, Emma started to feel easier about everything.

David opened the salon on his day off and gave Emma star treatment. Hours passed as she sat and he painstakingly cut and bound each strip of the long auburn hair, carefully placing the strips in the packing box, all the time quipping jokes and teasing her mercilessly. When he had finished she quite liked the new style, and it suited her cheeky face.

'Goodbye, Emma. I'll let you know when the wig is ready.'

And with that he stooped to kiss her.

One afternoon, when Emma was at home, she noticed a car draw up outside. David and his wife stepped out with a smart hatbox. The wig was ready. The manufacturers had left it uncut. An hour of cutting and styling later, he had finished, leaving her with a mop of her own red hair for the day when she would be bald.

Before leaving, David turned to her. 'If ever I had a daughter, I'd want someone like you, Emma.'

One stranger's kindness had helped her through the worst days of her illness so far.

As well as the matter of hair, there was the subject of school. Since the field trip Emma had not been attending school and was beginning to find the days at home long. She had recovered well from the second operation, her treatment had not yet started, and she was feeling bored.

One morning, Liz opened the door to a familiar face.

'Mr Fish?'

Sitting down with a cup of tea they began to reminisce. A good many years before (she didn't like to count!) he had been her RE teacher.

'I still remember the day, you know, when I had to reprimand a certain little girl for eating a sandwich under her desk after the bell had gone.'

Liz also remembered the day and the absolute horror of being discovered.

'Elizabeth, are you eating?'

'No, Sir?'

She had to copy out five hundred lines for her misdemeanour.

Now, apparently, as the head of home tutors for the county, he had come to discuss Emma's schooling.

'I would like Emma to have a tutor, to work with her at home and as she recovers from the treatment, eventually to work alongside her in school. I do have someone in mind, a Jill South. She's very nice. I think Emma will enjoy working with her.'

A meeting was arranged for the following week, before treatment was scheduled to begin. Emma took to Jill straight away, filling her in with a potted life history in minutes.

'I start radiotherapy tomorrow, Jill. The doctors say I probably won't be able to have lessons during the treatment, as I won't feel very well.'

Jill thought for a moment.

'Why not use this time to research a special project, then? You could write a book, covering all aspects of your illness, beginning with the radiotherapy visits.'

'Now that's an idea.'

So, camera in hand, Pete, Liz and Emma turned up for the first radiotherapy appointment. Dr Sinclair met with them all again. It was a much easier meeting. They weren't crying for a start, and this time Liz was a match for the consultant.

'Do you have any questions, Mr and Mrs Freeman?'

Quickly, she retorted, 'Is your cold better?'

Liz had taken patients to the unit years before as part of her nursing training and was prepared for the sight of the machines. Emma was wary, but Jill's idea helped. Everywhere she went she quizzed the staff as to their names and what they did. Liz stood all the time, Emma's shadow in the background, taking photographs. Very few child patients came through the department and the bright youngster looked as though she was going to spice things up a little.

Firstly, she was taken to meet Ben, the 'plaster cast man'. He was a stringy man, tall and wonderfully bendy, with dark hair and smiley eyes.

'Hello Emma, nice to meet you. I'll just explain quickly what I'll be doing with you.'

His job was to make a mask and suit for her, initially out of plaster of Paris, then out of a flesh-coloured plastic. She would wear this during each session. The mask would protect her face, and the suit her ovaries and uterus, while the radiation worked away at the tumour.

She lay still, feeling mummified, while he carefully placed bandage strips over her stomach, chest, shoulders and head until he had the right shape, leaving holes for her eyes, nose and mouth.

'That's great, Emma. I think I've finished with you for now. Good luck.'

Minutes later she was shown into the X-ray room. Inside was another white metal machine, this time with a movable head, able to direct finely measured beams of radiating ions at the body on the bed beneath.

Somewhat embarrassed, Emma undressed and lay face down, naked on the vast bed. Two radiotherapists began their task. With the aid of the computer hidden behind the screen they engraved precision pen marks on her diminutive body and head. The measuring process took almost an hour. The marks would have to remain on her body for the entire six weeks.

All the while, Liz was busy snapping away, glad of any distraction.

Eventually they were ready. The marks to guide the X-rays to her head and spine had been inked in position. The camera was lowered into place, like a metallic dinosaur swooping down on its prey. The treatment would last five minutes on her head and five minutes on her spine.

'You have to leave the room now, Mrs Freeman. We'll call you when we've finished.'

Outside, in the waiting room, Liz sat with Pete. In front of them was a beautiful table inset with a brass plaque: 'In memory of . . .' They stared together at the table. A plastic clock ticked infuriatingly on the wall overhead. 'It didn't do her much good, did it!' Pete remarked. They giggled together, not really knowing why. They were still waiting when one of the nurses beckoned them.

'I've got someone here who wants to see Emma?'

'We're just waiting for her now. She shouldn't be much longer.'

'Will you send her down when she comes out?'

One of the radiographers poked her head around the door.

'Mrs Freeman? We've finished with Emma. She can dress and go home now.'

Liz found her sitting up shakily on the bed. She felt a dull ache inside. She so wished she could go through the treatment for her, and this was only the beginning. 'Hey, guess what,' she said to Emma. 'There's a mystery person outside who wants to see you. Let's get these clothes on quickly and find out who it is.'

They reappeared in the corridor to find a rather large man. Emma stared at him for a while before shouting 'Mr Whittaker!' It was her headmaster, but minus his famous beard. Unknown to them he had Hodgkin's disease and was also in for radiotherapy.

Liz had nervously knocked on his office door not that long ago. Emma had returned home from school with a reading book containing blasphemy. She was not sure how the head would react to her complaint, but in she went. He was very gracious and thanked her for pointing it out to him. Collecting Emma later that day she noticed the school caretaker burning offending copies in the yard!

Mr Whittaker was thrilled to see the family. They exchanged news and he left, but not before he had invited them all to tea.

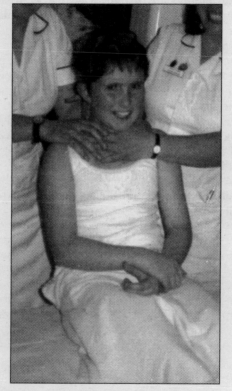

*Smiling through radiotherapy.*

# Chapter 7

'Emma, are you awake?'

Liz looked in to find her daughter staring at her pillow. On it were small flecks of hair. It had begun. Soon little patches were falling out in her comb and then simply in her hand. The hair on top of her head was the last to go. One morning she stood looking at her bald reflection in the mirror, her head as round and smooth as an egg.

The constant nausea made Emma's spirit sink even lower. The worst period seemed to be immediately after treatment. Pete took time off work to sit in the back of the car with her, tenderly holding her head as they weaved their way through traffic and her body heaved with the vomiting. Her appetite all but disappeared. Liz could not tempt her with anything and the weight was falling off her tiny frame.

'How about pancakes?' she offered one lunchtime, having ransacked the cupboards for ideas.

Emma's eyes lit up. Liz whisked up the rich batter, fried the pancakes, and smothered them with sugar and lemon juice. Within seconds Emma had demolished the lot, her taste buds springing into action. For the next six weeks she lived on nothing else. One uncle often dropped in on the pretext of seeing her, just to sample some!

At one morning's session, Alice, the department receptionist, noticed her patient's usual cheeriness had evaporated. 'Is Emma all right?' she whispered.

Liz explained they had had a particularly restless night with her and she was feeling a bit low. 'To be honest, we're finding it difficult to occupy her, Alice, she's feeling so sick.'

'Leave it to me,' she replied firmly.

Alice was something of a formidable character in the department. Liz thought of her as 'Honor Blackman', with her blonde bob, sultry eyes and curvaceous figure. She wondered what she was going to arrange.

The following morning Alice handed Emma a white doctor's coat, cut to size, complete with a name tag: 'Emma Freeman, Radiotherapy Department Helper'. Together they went on their rounds. That completed, Alice installed Emma behind the reception desk, instructing her to answer the phone, before leaving to root out doctors to telephone her 'new assistant'.

Emma was in her element. Her face beamed with importance. For the first time in weeks she forgot all about the sickness. At the end of her 'shift' Alice handed her an armful of paper containing long lists of patients' names. 'Now, Emma. I would like you to sort these names for me, listing them under the correct consultant. I just haven't got the time. Do you think you could do that for me?'

In the afternoons after treatment, Emma sat at home on the sofa, laboriously copying and sorting the names. Liz watched her frown with concentration, frequently crumpling a spoilt page and starting over again. It had to be perfect for Alice.

Each morning, Alice, glasses on the edge of her nose, would peer down at the list and exclaim loudly: 'You've saved me hours of work, Emma.'

The scam went on for weeks and Emma never did realise the lists were imaginary.

Halfway into the treatment they were due to honour their date for tea with the headmaster. By now, Emma didn't really want to go. Within the four walls of her home people were allowed to see her bald, but in the outside world things were different. Her wig was better than nothing, but it was still a wig: it was hot and itched incessantly.

'I don't know whether I want to go, Mum.'

'Come on, Emma. We'll have a lovely time. Why don't you wear your baseball cap instead? You look good in that.'

Mr Whittaker's house overlooked Langland Bay on the Gower coast. It was a glorious day, and they stopped momentarily to listen to the gentle lapping of the waves on the pebbly beach. He welcomed them in, noting Emma's unease instantly.

'Emma, would you come with me into the kitchen for a moment?'

The door closed behind them. He looked at her mischievously.

'Go on, you take your cap off and I'll take mine off!'

Before she knew it, the caps were off, and they were comparing bald heads! Everyone looked bemused at the varying sounds of hysteria emitting from the room.

Emma returned all smiles. Maybe being bald was not so bad after all.

By the end of the six weeks Emma was feeling well enough to write for her project. Poems came more naturally to her than prose and she composed dozens, some funny, some poignant.

She wrote about her hair:

As I grew up, my hair grew down
Longer day by day . . .

I used to wear it in different ways
With ribbons made of lace
My favourite way was a ponytail
To keep it off my face

'You must have your hair cut' the doctor said
Even though it was down to my waist . . .

She wrote about her mother:

But the best friend I'll have is my dear old Mum
Who's looked after me all these years
She's washed my face and changed my bottom
And kissed away all my tears

Other poems were simply funny, like 'Odd Ode':

This is the tale of Winnie Mouse
Who asked some friends round to her house
She cooked a lot of lovely food
To feed her friends and all her brood
When they were eating the lights went out
All the little ones began to shout
It looked as if it was the night
She lit a candle for some light
When the light came on again
They all said they had stomach pain
To their horror instead of broth
They had all been eating the tablecloth

But it was her poem 'Radiotherapy Unit' that revealed
the strength of character that had been growing so subtly
through the last few months of her illness. Emma had an

inoperable brain tumour, she had undergone major surgery, she had lost all her hair, but she was holding on to her sense of humour for dear life.

> At first I thought it was a bind
> To go there every day
> But all the girls they were so kind
> They send your nerves away.
>
> When you're new they show you around
> To put your mind at rest
> The big machines and different sounds
> They put you to the test . . .
>
> There's Ann and Pam and Mandy too
> Who'll tell you to undress
> 'Now lay there still and don't you move'
> Well, where would I go in my vest!
>
> They take blood from you by the armful
> And tell you not to worry
> I try to be good and cheerful
> Then get out of the place in a hurry
>
> When I finish I'll miss them all
> You see I've got used to the place
> I'll try to behave, I won't cry or bawl
> But wear a big smile on my face

Jill was so touched by the poem that she forwarded it to the local newspaper and they published it. Two women, moved by Emma's words, wrote to her: 'You are much in our hearts. God bless you, Emma darling. He will, I know. He takes much care of you. Don't forget that God always helps his children.'

God certainly seemed to be helping this child in a wonderful way.

*The inevitable hair loss.*

# Chapter 8

After what seemed like a lifetime, the radiotherapy sessions drew to an end. They knew a scan would follow and secretly were expecting a miracle. Churches throughout Swansea had organised special prayer meetings for Emma and everyone had been praying hard for her to be healed. Surely God was going to answer. Liz played the scene excitedly in her mind, Dr Sinclair looking at the scans in disbelief: 'I can't understand it, Mrs Freeman, the tumour seems to have disappeared.'

On the day of the scan they were confident the news would be good.

It wasn't. The consultant put the films up on the now-familiar light box for them to see. There was no change. No change at all. The tumour had not even shrunk by a millimetre.

He, at least, was pleased. 'The tumour has not grown or spread to Emma's spine and the radiotherapy will hopefully continue its effects for some time. I think she can be discharged. I will, of course, carry on monitoring her progress. We need to check her height and weight every three months. I am also concerned to see that she goes through puberty normally. And she will need a scan every year. But for now she is free to return to normal life.'

They left his room reeling, moving through the waiting room to the outer doors, finding the car, unlocking it.

How could they go back to normal life with the tumour still there, unchanged? What had gone wrong? Why hadn't God answered their prayers? Had they put Emma through this, the hair loss, vomiting, tiredness, the risks of complications, all for nothing?

Emma accepted the news quite casually. She was almost getting used to the old orange in her head. She had not been expecting any miracle really. By far the worst thing for her was the prospect of returning to normal life with no hair. Only the other day she had appeared in the doorway in tears. One of the older boys from the street had been taunting her. 'What's that you're wearing then, Freeman? Call that hair? It's a joke.'

Paul managed to make out through her sobs what had happened. Incensed, he ran out of the house and up the street. 'Don't you make fun of my sister!' he shouted, punching the boy hard on the nose.

The incident had left an ugly imprint in Emma's mind. That was just one boy. What would facing an entire class in school be like? She continued for a time with Jill's lessons at home but knew she would have to brave it soon.

In the middle of the summer term she went to school wearing both her baseball cap and wig. She would stay just for the morning session.

'Emma! Where have you been? We've really missed you!'

In seconds she was jumped on. Friends piled around her, bombarding her with questions. It was so good to see them again. Most she had not seen since the field trip. Everything was going to be fine.

In time she started to use the wig to tease people. One morning they were giving a neighbour a lift on their way to school. He had been away in the last year and knew nothing of her illness. He was teasing her and pulling the peak on her cap when, suddenly, her entire hair moved. There was a stunned silence before they all fell about laughing at his horrified face.

In many ways life did return to a level of normality. Pete was given the all-clear to drive again after nearly three years, which was one less pressure. Liz returned to her night shifts on the antenatal ward after over a year's absence. Emma was relaxed and happy in school. Paul was busy studying.

And yet things weren't normal. The tumour continued to dominate everything. Liz kept on wondering if she wasn't somehow to blame. In quieter moments she found herself sifting through memories of their early married life when the children were small for something, just something, to explain why this had happened to them. Perhaps somewhere they had stepped out of God's will.

They had relied on God to supply their needs all the time in the early days. She remembered one time vividly. Their first house was an old property and needed a new concrete floor. Her brother had agreed to help and they had measured and ordered the materials. It was a fine, crisp Saturday morning. They were halfway through the job when Pete realised he did not have enough cement. The builders' merchants had closed for the weekend and they had to finish the floor that day. He decided the only thing he could do was pray about it.

Half an hour later there was a knock at the door. Liz answered. A friendly face met her. 'I can see you're cementing, love. You couldn't use some ready mix could you? We've too much for our job and it has to be used today or it'll spoil.'

Within minutes bucketloads of cement were being brought through. There was enough to finish the floor, and they did so that day!

Almost all her early memories were the same. God was
with them constantly, supplying the smallest need. Pete
spent eleven months on sick leave at one point, three
months of it in bed downstairs. But God provided for
them. Someone would bring a joint of meat when money
was particularly short. Pete's parents would secretly fill
the children's money boxes on the kitchen window sill
when they needed new shoes. They lost count of the times
an envelope would come through the door containing a
gift to meet an unexpected bill.

As the children grew they considered moving. Their
house was on a busy main road, wedged between a
garage and a noisy pub and beer garden. There was little
space for the children to play. Midwives were in great
demand and Liz knew she would be able to go back to
work and choose her hours. So after nine years she had
returned.

Her first night had been dreadful. Her stomach turned
as she handled monitors and machines that had not even
existed when she trained. She had rushed home to take
the children to school before sinking into bed and into a
relieved sleep. At ten past three she woke with a start.
She had slept through the alarm. There was no time to
dress. She threw some clothes over her nightclothes and
ran for it. At the school two little waifs were standing,
hoods up, in the pouring rain, the teacher looking none
too pleased.

They had moved then into Hill Drive, a small bungalow
in a quiet street. Was it here that they had stepped out of
God's will? Was it here they had started to depend on
God less?

But she honestly did not feel driven by material desires.
Pete's mother would often remark how much she felt at
home there, to which Pete would laugh, 'You should do –
it's all your old furniture!'

Day after day she tossed past decisions over in her mind. Was this God's punishment for them? There seemed to be no release. Some nights she had strange and terrifying dreams. In one recurrent dream, she would be at Emma's funeral, watching the neat wooden coffin being lowered into the cold ground. She would wake up, bathed in clammy sweat.

Then Emma began to have unusual dreams. One morning at breakfast she said through a mouthful of toast: 'I had a strange dream last night, Mum. I saw lots of black horses. They were carrying something. I don't know what it was.' Black horses carried coffins. Now Emma was dreaming about funerals as well. Was she going to die soon? Was God preparing her for that day? Perhaps Dr Sinclair's bleak prognosis was going to come true after all. Perhaps she wouldn't survive into her teenage years?

Liz felt quite alone. There was her twin sister. There was Pete. But she felt unable to open up completely to anyone. If only her mother was still alive, perhaps things would have been different.

One morning their family GP called.

'I'm sorry, Emma's not here,' Liz said.

'Good, because I've come to see you,' she replied, and sat with her, allowing her to pour out her heart. She came often after that.

# Chapter 9

'What on earth is the matter, Liz?'

Pete looked up as his wife came through the door in tears. She was a blubbering mess. He sat her down and listened worriedly as she tried to relate a conversation she had just had with a friend in the local shopping centre.

'She asked me how Emma was, Pete, and I told her the tumour as far as we know is untreatable.' She started to cry again. He handed her some more tissues. 'She told me I was not trusting God. I should ask God to heal her and I should claim the promise in James 5.'[2]

Pete was aghast. This friend was a pastor's wife, from a large charismatic church. Had she really told Liz she was to blame for Emma not being healed?

'What did you say to her, Liz?'

'I told her we had asked God to heal her. She said that he would heal her then, and if we did not see it happen we did not have enough faith.'

'That's ridiculous.'

He took a Bible down from the bookcase and opened it.

'Look at the passage in James. We've done that. The elders have anointed Emma with oil. We have asked God

---

[2] James 5:13–16.

to heal her. We have got to leave it with him now. We have done our part. It's utter nonsense to say we haven't believed.'

The incident seemed to be the beginning. Soon all kinds of dubious help and advice were being forced in their direction.

Liz answered the telephone one morning to a complete stranger. He said he was from a church in Swansea. He had heard about their daughter. Could he and another man come to the house to lay hands on her? Pete snatched the phone from her. He thanked the man for his concern but they had already obeyed the command to lay hands within their own church.

Another morning an anonymous package arrived in the post. Inside they found a piece of white cloth. The sender told them the cloth had been 'blessed'. If they placed it on Emma's head it would heal the tumour.

Alternative therapies were the next phase. Someone suggested Emma try reflexology. An aunt suggested she try homeopathy.

A work colleague brought back a bottle of 'holy water' from Lourdes. She was so kind and so well meaning. In tears, she pleaded with Liz to take it for Emma. Liz found herself wondering what harm could come from it? She felt completely vulnerable, susceptible to anything that would bring some hope for her daughter.

All the time people seemed to be implying that their trust in God and in the medical profession was not enough. They should do more. At one point an uncle showed them an article from the *Reader's Digest* about a boy who had recovered from a brain tumour after an operation in the United States. After reading the piece Pete made an appointment to see Mr Beeston. He showed him the cutting.

'It's like this, Mr Beeston. We're desperate. Money is no object. If we need to find thousands, we'll do it somehow. Please just let me know if there is an operation somewhere that'll work for her?'

The surgeon shook his head. 'It's not a question of money, Mr Freeman, or even of another country. There is nothing we can do for her, nothing.'

At home again they came back to the fact they were dependant upon God, on him alone, and on whatever he had planned for Emma. Nobody else could help.

As the New Year opened, the crisis strangely seemed over. It was almost as if the last torrid year, the field trip, the operation, the radiotherapy, had not happened. Emma steadily regained her health. She had been attending school full time for months now. Her hair had grown back, in tufts at first. It was a different colour, less red, and nothing would grow over the scars from the shunt operations, but it was hair and it was her own. As soon as she had a respectable covering, Liz had packed the wig away, deep in the cupboard, hidden among the paraphernalia of her toys and clothes.

Hospital appointments were sporadic now and merely check-ups. The steroid medication had stopped months ago. The only physical reminder of the radiation was the grey pile of cardboard sick trays mouldering in the garden shed.

One morning Pete's sister dropped in to see them.

'Would you like a cup of coffee, Sue?'

'Oh, I'd love one, thanks. Is Emma around anywhere? I've got something for her.'

Emma bounded in from the garden. She loved her aunt's visits.

'Look at this, Emma. They were given out in church on Sunday. He's coming to Swansea soon and he's supposed to be a very good speaker. Do you fancy coming along with me?'

Emma glanced through the leaflet – 'Tell Wales Campaign with Luis Palau' – as her mother and aunt chatted seamlessly through the comforting mundane details of families and shared lives.

'It's going to be held in the Morfa Stadium next month,' said Sue. 'Thousands are expected to attend. It should be quite an experience.'

'Yes, I'll come with you, Aunty Sue, why not.'

'Great. I'll book the tickets then.'

On the night they set off early to find a good seat, but not early enough. The stadium was heaving with people. They found seats at the back, to the left of the stage area. They could see the platform, a tiny slither in the distance.

For an evening in the middle of June, it was freezing. Emma squeezed up close to her aunt, glad she had brought an extra jumper with her. The meeting started. The musicians struck up the first hymn, 'How Great Thou Art'. She had only ever been to small churches: Lonlas Mission when she was a toddler, Dynefor Road Mission now. She had not heard singing like this before – thousands of voices, rising and filling the stadium.

Luis Palau stood up, a cream-suited figure. She could see him in the distance if she squinted her eyes. She could just discern his words through the strange Argentinian accent. He was speaking of God's love. He told the expectant crowd they were sinners, but God had sent Jesus to die for them.

The words were familiar ones. She had heard them before. They constructed her earliest memories . . . Sunday school . . . Sunshine Corner. Her tender life had been saturated in the story of Jesus. Her father often used to joke about their godly births – she had been born during the weekly prayer meeting, her brother during Sunday school. She believed in Jesus for herself. She had never known a time when she had not believed. Her mother told her that when she was four she had prayed, asking Jesus to forgive her sins. Why then did the message seem to affect her tonight?

Luis Palau carried on preaching, the words reaching her almost in slow motion, until it was as if she was the only one in the stadium – herself with God. The truth gripped her. She knew she was a sinner. She had not realised she was such a sinner until tonight. Jesus had died to give her – Emma Freeman – eternal life.

The sermon ended. She heard Luis Palau calling people to the front to give their lives to Jesus.

'I'm going, Aunty Sue.'

She brushed past her aunt, down the steps, in among the hundreds of others, to the grassed pitch. A counsellor found her and prayed with her, pushing a leaflet into her hand. All around her she felt an overwhelming sense of joy. Jesus had died for her; given her everlasting life. She had always known it. Tonight she felt it.

They did not say much in the car on the way home. Her aunt did not want to make a fuss. She had felt for a long time that her niece was a Christian. Perhaps this was God giving Emma a special assurance, an opportunity to commit herself to him completely. Sue dropped her outside the house.

Over mugs of scalding hot chocolate Pete and Liz listened to her animatedly recount the events of the evening, eyes shining – the singing, the preaching, going forward to commit herself to Christ. They knew God had been with her since her early infant days. He had given her grace to cope with all that the last two years had brought. But for some reason he had spoken to her in a unique way that night and given her an unmistakable experience of repentance and faith in Jesus.

With Emma restored to health physically and spiritually, they spent a week holidaying in the Norfolk Broads on a barge boat with Mar and Dyfrig, deciding this time to give any ferries a miss! The weather was warm and the days languid as they glided through the silken country-side.

Emma spent the time mostly with her aunt. They were both frightened of mooring and, wrapped in their life jackets, would drop below at the appropriate time, eyes shut, until it was safe to reappear.

Paul, in the meantime, had taken up fishing with intense seriousness. Every morning without fail he would take his place on top of the barge and set up his fishing tackle, waiting for the elusive bite. Every night he would reel in his rod dejectedly. Dyfrig and Pete teased him endlessly. On the final day of the holiday, flat on his back in the sun, Dyfrig lazily pulled at the line. 'Oh I think he's finally caught something, Pete. Reel it in Paul!' Out of the water emerged an orange plastic goldfish, looking sadly up at him.

It was a glorious week and they returned sunburnt and refreshed, ready for the new school year.

In September Emma started her first term at compre-hensive school. They had informed the headmaster of her brain tumour but, amidst the jostling crowds, she was just another nervous first former. Nothing about her stood out particularly. Her hair had grown into a pretty bob. Only close friends from primary school remembered her illness. A few vaguely recalled the ginger wig and baseball cap she had worn for a while, but thought nothing more of it.

She was advised not to take part in netball and other hard sports but she was allowed to swim, and she excelled at it, pushing herself through the school's icy pool, length after length, feeling healthier and stronger by the minute.

Her twelve-year-old body was changing too, crossing the tender divide between girl and woman. In October the clearest sign of puberty at last arrived. Liz sat, mother with daughter, gently explaining things to her, inwardly thrilled.

Puberty had arrived entirely naturally. The six weeks of radiation had not affected her ovaries or pituitary gland after all. There would be no need for damaging hormone treatments.

They knew the tumour was still there, of course, the lingering mass in the centre of her brain, but then according to the doctors it had always been there. The shunt was working away subtly to reduce fluid build-up and headaches. Radiotherapy had hopefully stopped the tumour in its tracks, although it hadn't reduced it in size. No doctor had ever been able to prove it was cancerous.

Perhaps that brief crisis, when life seemed to crash around them, was it. A brief, momentary alarm bell, warning them not to take life for granted, forcing them to keep trusting in God.

Maybe God did have longer plans for Emma Freeman's life, beyond the oncologist's pessimistic predictions.

The year 1990 opened with disturbing news on another front. It seemed their home was subsiding under them!

Years before, as they moved into Hill Drive, Pete's father had remarked with a definite note of gloom: 'I don't like the look of that crack up there.' Pete had taken little notice, filling it in and painting over it. He did the same with the other cracks that appeared sporadically around the house.

In time Liz had found herself sweeping up piles of cement dust outside the back door, dust coming, it seemed, from the gaping crevices emerging in the outer walls. Finally the guttering had dropped. The noise of the rainwater spilling from the roof had kept Liz awake one night too many. 'I think it's time we got someone in to have a look, Pete.'

The surveyor had had a similar note of doom in his voice as he inspected the property: 'Your house appears to be sinking, I'm afraid.' He had set up a series of weights and left with the foreboding words, 'I'll be back in two years.'

The two years were now up and it was not looking good. Test results had proved the foundations were completely inadequate and the bungalow was slipping slowly into them. Remedial work would cost over thirty thousand pounds, more than the value of the bungalow when they had bought it. It would entail a massive engineering operation. They would have to strip the house to a shell. All the floors would have to come up. Huge pipes would be inserted and seven tons of concrete pumped through each one.

Their insurance company agreed to meet the costs of the work. They would have to find somewhere to live in the meantime and somewhere to put the entire contents of their home.

Everybody in the church rallied to help in the latest crisis. A good friend arranged for them to stay in an empty house used occasionally to house missionaries back from furlough, and they moved in, along with their carpets, fireplaces, bathroom and kitchen, on the last day of August.

Each day they dropped by to check on the engineers' progress, feeling like archaeologists on an excavation sight. The bungalow was barely recognisable. Pete's mother stood looking at the rubble around her: 'Oh Liz, look at your home.'

Liz found herself amazingly good-humoured. After all they had been through with Emma, this was nothing: bricks and mortar, a little inconvenience.

As winter approached the last engineer left. Women from the church came to help clean and men to lay carpets. Liz's brother repainted for them. By November they were back home.

Perhaps now their shifting world would settle, along with their home.

# Chapter 10

It was Christmas morning 1991. Emma woke early, feeling the bulging stocking in her bed with palpable excitement. She squinted at the alarm clock – still only four o'clock. She had hours to wait before waking everyone else. She lay in the milky darkness clutching the stocking. There was something magical about Christmas morning: the smell of pine needles and satsumas; comforting, timeless family traditions. She stole a chocolate coin, glinting at her in its gold wrapper, rolled over and tried to go back to sleep.

By seven o'clock the house was up, everyone in dressing gowns and slippers crouched around the tree, ripping packages open until the carpet was a sea of torn paper. The ceremony over, they slouched, enjoying the mess, distractedly watching the early-morning films.

Pete yawned. 'I told Mum we'd be there mid-morning. Perhaps we'd better get dressed.'

One by one they moved, slow as sea slugs.

In the bedroom, Emma suddenly felt a wave of tiredness engulf her. She felt sick. Perhaps it was the chocolate she had eaten. She shook herself and pulled her clothes on. She loved going to her grandparents for Christmas lunch – her grandmother made the most delicious roast. She would feel better soon.

'Happy Christmas! Come on in.'

They trooped into the house, cosy and full of the smell of turkey already. Pete's father gave Emma a great bear hug. She looked so grown up these days, turning into quite a young lady. He noticed she was quieter than usual.

They gathered around the table, pulled crackers, groaned at appalling jokes, and then quietness descended as they devoured the meal. Emma sat putting the food into her mouth with difficulty. She couldn't taste a thing. Slowly she pushed the food into a mound on her plate and looked up. They were bringing the pudding to the table now, a great bulging pudding. 'I feel a bit sick, Gran.'

Her grandmother looked over at her. 'You do look pale. Why don't you go and have a lie down on the sofa?'

The feast over, they surveyed the debris in the kitchen. A turkey carcass poked its head above the piles of gravy-stained dishes and soiled pans. Liz tried to clear a little space. 'Do you think she's all right, Pete?'

'She'll be fine – too much excitement and chocolate, probably.'

It was Christmas day, and yet here Liz was, wondering if this was the beginning of another crisis. Stupid really. Emma had been fine for almost three years now.

After an hour on dish duty, they emerged. Emma was sitting up and feeling better. Liz glanced at her watch. There was enough time to watch some television before going home. She was on duty tonight: she had drawn the short straw at work yet again. As full and fat as stuffing balls, they spread out for the afternoon.

Later on they said their goodbyes and piled into the car for home, snaking through the silent streets.

Pete saw to the children as Liz got ready for work. She would be back by eight o'clock in the morning. After a scant sleep they were spending Boxing Day with her niece and family.

'Good night, Emma. Was it a good Christmas Day?'

'It was great, Mum, great.'

Pete stirred again. Perhaps he should get up. He had woken briefly when Liz had returned but soon dozed off again. He could hear Paul moving around and got up to join him. They ate breakfast in hushed tones.

'We'll let Emma sleep on for a bit.'

Ten o'clock came and went, half past ten – still no sign of her. Pete started to feel a little uneasy. She had never slept this late before. It was almost eleven o'clock now.

'I'll just look in on her.'

He put his nose into the room.

'Emma. Are you awake?'

There was no answer. She was still. He went to the bed, sat by her side, his hand on her cheek.

'Emma. Are you awake?'

Still no response – she was in a deep sleep. He tried again, louder and more urgent. By now there was fear in his eyes. Something was wrong, very wrong. He would have to wake Liz.

Liz turned over. She could hear Pete saying something. He wouldn't wake her now. He knew she'd just gone to bed. She felt his face over hers, his voice clearer now.

'It's Emma. I can't wake Emma.'

She sat up with a start. Throwing on her dressing gown she ran into the room. She cradled her daughter's still body in her arms, yanked her upright, all the time shouting, 'Emma, Emma!'

Finally Emma responded. Her eyes opened. Liz felt a cold weight fall in her chest. One of her pupils was dilated like a large shiny black button.

'I feel . . . a bit . . . sick, Mum.'

Her words were slow, slurred, like a drunk. She needed to be seen by somebody urgently.

'It's all right, Emma. You're going to be all right. Dad's gone to call a doctor. We'll just get some clothes on you.'

She found her jumper on the floor, and some jeans. Emma sat on the bed like a rag doll.

'Put your leg in, Emma, that's right.'

Her movements were lumbering, clumsy. This was taking forever – what was Pete doing?

Outside the room, Pete was in a panic. It was Boxing Day. All surgeries would be closed. He could try ringing 999. He decided to ring the children's ward in the city hospital. Ruth had been transferred there now. She would know what to do. The phone rang a few times and he was through.

'Is that Ruth? It's Pete Freeman. There's something wrong with Emma. What should we do?'

The familiar voice on the end of the line was calm, reassuring. 'Bring her up to the ward straight away, Pete. We'll be waiting for you.'

He replaced the receiver. His hand was shaking. He could hear Emma's strange speech from the other room, and Liz's voice, agitated. He rang his niece to explain they wouldn't be joining them for lunch. They offered to come and fetch Paul for him.

'That's so kind, so kind.'

Within minutes they had picked Paul up.

At last Emma was ready. Liz helped her into the car and, as quickly as he could, Pete drove. She was getting worse by the minute. In his mirror, Pete could see her left eyelid starting to droop. Liz held on to her tightly as the car swept along deserted streets, jaded decorations hanging in shop fronts.

There were few cars in the hospital grounds. They led Emma up the steps with difficulty, found a wheelchair, and pushed her to the children's ward. Ruth was there at the door to meet them.

'This is Oliver. He's going to take a look at Emma for you.'

Minutes later, Oliver emerged from the side room.

'I'm afraid there is little I can do for her. She should be seen by a neurological specialist immediately – in casualty. Do you know how to get there?'

'We know,' Pete replied. 'We'll take her there now.'

Ruth helped them put Emma back into the wheelchair and watched them leave. Emma was very poorly. She hoped this was not the end.

In the car Pete berated himself for his mistake – if he had only taken her to casualty first of all. The journey there now would take half an hour. He prayed the delay had not made things worse.

Emma lay against her mother saying something softly: 'So tired . . . Mum . . . I . . . want to . . . sleep.'

They sped into the second hospital car park. It was quiet. They imagined other families, other normal families in their homes, feasting on cold turkey and pickles, handing around half-eaten boxes of chocolates.

What was happening to their daughter?

In casualty Emma was examined immediately by the registrar, as Mr Beeston was on holiday. He said very little, started her on a high dose of steroids, and sent her for a scan.

'I'll speak with you when I've seen the results, Mr and Mrs Freeman.'

It was early afternoon by the time they returned from the scan room, and Emma was exhausted. The sister found them a small private room on the neurology ward. They waited there while Emma slept.

At four o'clock they were asked to attend an interview with the registrar. It was the moment they had been dreading. Pete quietly put his arm around his wife as they walked to the interview room, all the time praying, 'Lord, help. Please, help.'

The registrar was very calm and they hung on his every word, his every look. Pete sat immobile, the words hurting every atom in his body. 'He can't mean that our Emma has had a bleed, a stroke, that the eyesight in her left eye has been affected,' thought Pete. 'After all, it's Christmas. It's Boxing Day. Surely it's the time of good cheer. Not this terrible news.' The registrar steadily continued. 'He can't mean the tumour has grown,' Pete thought. 'This can't be happening to Emma, our darling daughter. After all, she's been fine, but this – no. It can't be happening again.'

They left the room stunned. The tumour was looming large in their world again, this time causing paralysis. They had known, of course, that it was a stroke. Liz was a nurse. Pete had worked in the ambulance service and later as a theatre technician. They knew the signs. Denial was a strange thing. What would they tell Emma now? How would they explain this to her?

Emma was awake when they returned. She lay in yet another hospital bed, her eyes blank. She sensed this news was the most serious to date. She felt strange. She had done since waking. Something was wrong with her eyes. The world was a blur. She was seeing two of everything around her – fuzzy, disjointed pictures. She couldn't move her right arm and leg properly. Her head ached.

She strained again to make out her parents' faces. Her mother's eyes were red, puffy. Her father's face was grey.

She heard them saying something about a 'bleed'. She decided she would be strong for them. Mustering all her strength, she forced out the words she wanted to say: 'Don't worry . . . everything will be all right. Let's just get on with it . . . and make me better.'

Outside in the corridor Pete picked up a pen and began to write. Years before an aged pastor had told him if he ever found himself unable to pray he should write his thoughts to God down. He could not pray. He was too angry with God. He had too many questions. And so he sat alone, writing furiously.


Liz had only slept for two hours since Christmas morning. She felt her body almost crumple under her.

'Why don't you go home, Liz? I'll stay with Emma tonight.'

'No. I want to stay with her. Can you take me home to just pick up a few things for tonight?'

At home, the front door closed behind them. Liz went straight to Emma's room. On the floor were her presents from the day before in a muddled heap. Instinctively, she went to tidy them. She picked up one of her new cuddly toys, held it against her, lent against the bed and wept.

She didn't hear the doorbell. Paul had returned from his cousin's house. He looked into Emma's room. He could see his mother, sitting on the bed, moaning in grief. He swallowed. He had never seen her cry like this before. He had to leave her alone. And yet he couldn't leave her alone. Drawing breath, he let himself in, sitting helplessly as she collapsed on his bony shoulders.

His father's voice broke into the stillness of the room. 'Liz, Mar said she'll stay with you and Emma tonight. She'll come and collect you now, if that's all right.'

Liz looked at her son, who in a brief moment of time seemed to have become a man.

'Tell her that's fine.'

Half an hour later they were back in the hospital. Emma was sleeping soundly. There was no change in her condition. Trying to make as little noise as possible, they made up the makeshift beds and changed into nightclothes. Liz lay on the floor on one side of Emma and Mar on the other. Exhausted, they drifted off to sleep.

In the middle of the night Mar let out a sudden, terrifying scream. Something was on her face; something light, feathery. She groped in the darkness for the light switch, whispering frantically: 'Liz, I think there's a huge spider in the room.'

The lights on, they discovered the culprit – a faded Christmas decoration had fallen from the ceiling!

*Pete, Liz, Emma and Paul at a family wedding
– months before the strokes.*

# Chapter 11

In the morning they found out that Mr Beeston was not due back until New Year's Eve. In the meantime the registrar wanted to keep Emma on intensive steroid medication.

She was very weak. She lay in bed, barely moving, her left eyelid completely closed up. The registrar explained with abstract fascination that, because of the stroke and the damage to the eye Emma was experiencing ptosis: 'When double vision occurs suddenly the brain immediately closes one eye up, including the eyelid.'

It didn't help to know. He could explain what was happening easily enough but seemed to have no answers.

In the meantime visitors were starting to arrive, startled by the girl they found in the hospital bed, taken aback by the suddenness of her relapse. A favourite uncle was so upset, he told Liz as he left: 'If anything happens to that girl, I'll never darken the doors of a church again.'

'Den,' she replied, 'you don't darken the doors of a church now, and you never have!'

'That's true enough,' he mused.

Of all the visitors Paul was the most faithful. He was in his GCSE year, studying hard for mock exams, and the darts world championship was on, another attraction. But every day he would come in and sit by Emma's bed, often when she was sleeping, for hours at a time, stroking her limp arm. She would wake intermittently, rambling in half sleep. Her mind seemed to be hallucinating. Often she would cry out that she could hear horses galloping through the hospital corridors.

One evening she woke, drowsily, to find Paul at her side again. Ever since he could remember she would pester him, saying, 'Paul, do you love me?' He would never reply. This evening, in the middle of her mutterings, she asked clearly, 'Paul do you love me?'

He carried on stroking her arm. He couldn't mess around now. 'Yes,' he muttered beneath his breath. 'Yes, I love you.'

Content, she wandered back into sleep.

Mr Beeston met with them on his first day back. Immediately he gave them a talking-to for not bringing Emma straight to his department. They knew he reacted because he cared, but his words dealt another blow to their already fragile spirits.

The chastisement over, he went through the finer points of Emma's deterioration with them. He explained that the new, growing part of the tumour had started to bleed, causing the stroke. He was beginning to think she should see another specialist.

'One of the London hospitals is pioneering surgery for tumours that are impossible to operate on – a procedure known as "stereo tactic radio surgery". This involves inserting antennae into the tumour and then passing radium pellets through the antennae. It is in its early stages but it might be Emma's best option. If you agree, I will write to enquire whether she would be a suitable candidate. In the meantime, I have arranged further tests for her.'

With Emma he was kinder. He had not seen her for a few years now. Her regression was shocking. He explained simply what had been happening in her head and outlined the possibility of more surgery. He noticed a new nervousness appearing.

'Pretend I'm Paul Daniels, Emma. Whatever I say, say, "Yes, Paul".'

She looked up at him trustingly: 'Yes, Paul.'

Whatever the surgeon suggested she would try.

That afternoon she was taken for an angiogram. A catheter would be inserted through her femoral artery and dye fed through the catheter. The procedure would highlight the tumour and surrounding vessels. She would need a general anaesthetic.

Outside the room Emma was anxious: 'I won't have to have any needles, will I?'

A large Caribbean doctor opened the door. 'Hello, Emma – I'm going to give you the needle.'

Usually brave about such things, she felt tears starting to well in her eyes.

'Don't cry. Everybody will have the pinprick.'

'Well, you have it then!' she quipped

New Year's Day came and went. Liz missed the celebrations, the famous Big Ben chimes, hidden away as she was from the outer world in Emma's miniscule room. She spent every day and night with her.

On the 7th January, in the afternoon, she noticed Emma seemed even more tired than usual. She found a nurse and voiced her concern. 'Emma seems awfully sleepy?'

The nurse promised to take a look at her in a while. When she did so, she observed that her left eye was more dilated. 'I'll go and get the doctor.'

He came by unhurriedly and checked her. He was fairly dismissive. 'I don't want to give her any more steroids, Mrs Freeman. Let's just see how she goes.'

At visiting time she unloaded her worries on Pete. Emma was so still, so quiet. She barely said a word all the time Pete was there.

'I don't see what we can do, Liz. The doctor has seen her and feels everything is all right.' He looked at his wife's drawn face, crippled with worry and exhaustion. 'Do you want me to stay with you tonight?'

'No, it's all right. You go home. I'll see you tomorrow.'

As soon as he left, Liz felt the uneasiness grip her. She didn't want to interfere, but she was convinced something was wrong. It was almost ten o'clock when Dawn dropped by the bed – she was another good friend from Lonlas Mission. A nurse on the intensive care ward, she was about to start a night shift. Liz confided in her. 'Dawn, I'm really concerned. Emma seems so sleepy.'

Dawn glanced at her charts. 'I'll go and have a quick word before I start my shift.'

Moments later the nurse came by to give Emma her nightly medication. She tried to wake her. 'Emma? Wake up, Emma. Wake up.' There was no response. She tried again, her face tense, concentrated.

Liz could barely utter the words. 'What's the matter?'

'I think she's unconscious, Liz. I'll call the doctor now.'

Liz looked at her daughter's serene face; she was sleeping like a baby. Was this it, the moment she had been steeling herself against all these years?

The doctor was summoned again. This time he acted with urgency. The nurse moved Liz outside the room. Her first instinct was to ring Pete, but he had only just left to go home. 'Please be in, Pete. Please be in,' she thought as she dialled their number. She could hear the doctor's frantic voice shouting 'Emma, wake up. Emma, wake up.' She got through. He was home.

'I'll be straight there, Liz, hang on.'

By the time he arrived, breathless, with Paul, there had been no change. Emma was still unconscious. They followed the ever-growing group of doctors and nurses as they wheeled her for another scan. Numbly they stood outside the room trying to decipher the muffled voices within. They heard one doctor's voice rise with panic. 'We'll try one last injection of steroids.'

There was a chilling silence. 'Emma can you hear me?'

They could make out her faint voice. 'Yes . . . yes . . . I can hear you.'

The doctor emerged with haunted eyes. 'She'll have to go into intensive care tonight.'

Dawn would be looking after her.

That night Pete and Liz slept in the hospital in Emma's room. Paul had gone home with his aunt. They would face the night and whatever it brought together. They knew that nearby Emma was somehow fighting for her life. Dawn came in constantly, peering into the room, whispering 'She's all right', and then leaving to keep vigil over her.

Pete lay on the floor agonising over the last days. He had written it all to God and he went over and over it now: 'Deep down in my soul I know that God cares about Emma and loves her with an everlasting love that is so great and victorious . . . the shock is awful, sickening and I feel the sense of uselessness large in my mind . . . she has constantly showed that her faith is in him who orders the stars into place, who set the plan of salvation for sinful man . . . what if . . . what's next . . . Oh Lord, please don't let her be worse.' He gave it all over to his God now. He could do nothing else. Emma's future was in the Maker's hands.

They woke with the first cold wintry rays and went stiffly to intensive care. Dawn had gone home. Emma, lying amidst the tubes and wires, was stable. There had been no further bleeds. The next twenty-four hours, however, would be critical.

At home, Dawn was in a terrible state. It had been too much. All night she had prayed as she had never prayed before, desperate that God should spare this little girl. She could not even explain to her bewildered mother. She laid her head on the kitchen table and cried.

# Chapter 12

'Liz, you really should eat something, come on.' Pete managed to steer her in the direction of the hospital canteen. He ordered some toast and coffee and they sat going through the motions of the meal as people milled around them.

They had barely slept. Liz felt her head pounding with tiredness. She ached to run away from stifling hospital rooms, the smell of sickness everywhere, the perpetual artificial lights. Her body felt grimy. How were they going to get through this day?

The caffeine helped to wake them a little. They left most of the toast. It was stale, like chewing cardboard. They walked back in silence.

The lights in the intensive care unit were dimmed, throwing into relief the flickering jagged lines on the machinery. Each bleep, each pulse, represented Emma's refusal to give up on life. They had not spoken to anyone in great depth about the events of last night. They presumed Emma had suffered another stroke. Looking now at the young girl lying heavily sedated they could see its cruel effects. It had run through her body like a whirlwind, leaving in its wake paralysis. The muscles on the right side of her face had dropped, leaving her with a strange twisted expression. Her right arm and leg, devoid of life, hung limply.

The critical twenty-four hours crawled to an end. Emma continued to be stable. There had been no further bleeds. She would be returning to the ward.

No longer sedated, Emma lay looking up at them with petrified eyes.

Mr Beeston came to see them the next morning. He looked at the couple sitting by Emma's bed, hunched like a pair of timid animals. He could only begin to imagine the despair they felt. They were truly a remarkable couple. In all his years in the hospital he had witnessed the worst in people: couples fighting, venting their frustrations on themselves and the staff. This couple was always so polite, with each other and with Emma, always so grateful to the doctors. It was astonishing really. He wished he had good news to tell them.

'Now then, Mr and Mrs Freeman. In view of what has happened to Emma in the last eleven days I think we need to look again at this tumour. I recommend we send her for an MRI scan. This is more sensitive and should give us a highly detailed picture of the progress of the tumour. You realise, of course, that time is of the essence. Unfortunately there are only two MRI scanners in the country and we have to wait for an appointment. I have stressed to them the urgency of the situation. I'm afraid all we can do is to wait, and monitor her in the meantime.'

One afternoon a work colleague of Pete's came in to see Emma. It was a short visit. Afterwards as Pete walked with him to the car he broke down. 'How on earth can you believe in God after this, Pete?'

Pete looked at him helplessly, trying to explain, trying to find the right words. 'It's like this. No one can help really. The medical people haven't any real answers. Who can we go to? We're driven to God, not away from him.'

Within days they heard that one of the hospitals had re-arranged its schedule and would be able to scan Emma that day. Excitedly they broke the news. But the little girl who once refused to be daunted was now terrified. She could not understand what was happening to her body. She seemed to be losing control of the most basic functions. She could not see properly, move her arm or leg, or even smile as she had done before. Now they wanted to take her out of hospital. The thought of going in an ambulance was abhorrent. She started to panic. 'I don't want to go in an ambulance . . . I want Gran and Grandpa with me.'

Liz watched as her daughter broke down. She held her, trying to soothe the terrors she was having. 'I know it's horrible, Emma. You've been so brave up till now. Please try to be strong. Why don't I see if we can all travel by car? Would that be all right?'

They managed to calm her while Pete went to pick up his parents. The car was loaded up to the hilt, the hospital wheelchair in the boot, Emma propped up on pillows between her worried grandparents.

Within an hour they arrived at the hospital and were directed to the scanning room. From her wheelchair Emma had her first glimpse of the rare machine. It would scan her entire body in minute detail, using magnetic fields.

She felt two radiographers lift her useless body strongly from the chair. They laid her on her back and fastened several thick straps to keep her in place. She looked up into a metal cage and grimaced as they placed it over her face, like some trapped rodent.

'The helmet has two speakers in it, Emma. If you need to say something urgently you can do so from within the scanner. Otherwise you must try not to speak. We need you to be as still as possible.'

Liz, looking on, could sense her daughter's fear. 'How long will she be in the scanner?' she asked.

The radiographer, intent, didn't look up. 'It should take about four and a half hours. We'll probably let her out halfway through for a short break.'

Liz winced.

Slowly, Emma felt herself move. The noise started up, a rhythmic, monotonous noise, gaining in momentum and volume. With grotesque slowness her body inched its way deep into the tunnel. Hours later only her feet were visible. Liz held them with every ounce of energy she could muster. She sang her customary stock of hymns and choruses, praying constantly. 'Lord, please be with her. Be near to her now.' Her arms ached.

Inside the tunnel, Emma kept her eyes shut. She tried to distract herself by listening to her mother's songs or imagining she was somewhere else. But nothing would rid her of the feeling that she was buried alive in this grim metal graveyard.

'Only minutes left now and it'll be over.'

Drained, with the noise of the machine battering their ears, they returned to the ward.

Mr Beeston met with them the following day.

'The MRI scan pictures have helped us to clarify the situation slightly. They reveal a second lesion, confirming the tumour is bleeding, causing the strokes. I realise that in itself this does not help a great deal. However, I do have good news. I have made further enquiries and it seems Emma is a suitable candidate for the stereo tactic surgery. Mr Gilbert, the consultant overseeing the programme, is the best in his field. As soon as he has an available space he will be in touch with us.'

At last there seemed to be some granule of hope, and yet Emma was so weak, her body so devastated by the strokes. Liz wanted to know what they could do for her now. She asked tentatively: 'What will happen with her in the meantime?'

'Well, for now she is stable, and we have to hope there will be no further bleeds. We will keep an eye on her on the ward, but in due course she will be able to go home.'

And so they were in this place again – more enforced waiting, and no answers.

Emma did appear to be regaining her strength after almost a fortnight of lying motionless through the Christmas and New Year holidays.

'I think it's time we tried to get you up, Emma,' the ward sister commented the next morning. She picked up both her legs firmly and swung them to the edge of the bed. 'You stand behind her, Liz, and support her pelvis.'

With considerable effort they managed to get Emma to stand. The blood rushed to her head and she felt herself sway precariously.

'Don't worry, we've got you. Try to move your left leg first of all.'

Emma put her left leg in front of the other, a movement she had carried out unconsciously since her early toddler days, only to find she had nothing to balance on: the muscles in her other leg were useless. She fell clumsily on to her mother. This was not going to be easy.

'Good, now move your right leg.'

How was that possible? It seemed redundant, as if it no longer belonged to her body. She strained every possible muscle she could find. She could see it had moved a little, although she wasn't able to really feel anything.

'Great, Emma, that's great.'

She had taken two steps, two measly steps. They helped her back into bed.

'We'll try again later.'

By the end of the day she had managed the few yards to the toilet and back. A day later she made it to the end of the ward. Soon she was able to make a few laps, but only with her mother supporting her, and only with the most strenuous effort.

From her bed she watched the haze of doctors and nurses darting around the ward, the visitors appearing and disappearing. She had been like that only weeks ago. Simple physical acts now seemed huge hurdles. She had to find another way of dressing, walking and eating using limbs that had broken down.

And then there was the matter of her eyesight. They had broken the news that her double vision was permanent. Apparently the stroke had caused 'irreparable damage to the third cranial nerve'. To add insult to injury she would be fitted with bulbous glasses.

She didn't really voice her hopelessness. Outwardly she was cheerful, sweet and eager to persevere. She wasn't the only one covering up.

As each day ended and Emma remained basically the same, Liz grew more despondent. The doctors would only say cautiously that she would 'improve'. But Liz had nursed people with strokes, nursed her own mother, and she knew that if a stroke was mild patients usually regained their physical abilities very quickly. Emma was so slow – would she ever walk properly again, would she ever run or swim?

Christmas morning seemed unreal now. She kept a snapshot of Emma in her mind, in her pink dressing gown, ripping open her parcels, barely glancing at the presents, as usual – she was always in such a rush. She stopped herself. She always *used* to be in such a rush.

The nights were harrowing. Liz watched Emma, listening to her every sound, fearing another bleed. She would wake in the early hours convinced that Emma had stopped breathing. She would wait for sounds of her warm breath before going back down. She would hear the nurses coming in to change over shifts, the medicine trolleys coming round. Then it would be daylight and their gruelling routine would start over again.

# Chapter 13

At the beginning of February Emma was allowed home permanently. She had not seen the outside world properly since Christmas Day. She looked on it now with such different eyes. The car pulled up outside their house. She could see two shifted images of the home she loved, one blurred, one clear. She waited for her father to remove the wheelchair from the boot and clumsily pull it together. She watched him reach into the car as he hoisted her body into the chair, aware that neighbours' eyes were on them. Slam. They were inside.

It was good to be home after the aridness of hospital life, but hard. This was the place she used to bound around, throwing doors open with careless abandon, the one place she would pile on to the floor to mooch or read. Now she had to stagger from one sitting place to another. She tried to get the hang of the chair, gingerly wheeling around, banging into doors and furniture on the way, but it felt so alien.

Liz was uneasy. The chair seemed to have 'disabled' imprinted on it. She wanted Emma to fight, to walk, not to rely on this.

Somehow they had to find a new way of living: they had to nurse her but inspire her to recovery also. Liz had contacted her employers within the first few days of Emma's stroke to tell them she would not be coming in now. Pete decided to work shortened days. Paul was studying for his GCSEs and was at home a lot of the time. So they drew together, cocooned in a safe home, subconsciously blocking out the other harmful world of tumours and radiation treatments.

Pete bought a leather-bound notebook and started a diary with Emma of each day, recording every infinitesimal incident, the nature of every meal, and the name of every visitor. On the 18th February he wrote down for her: 'Moved my arm up above my head . . . on my own!' Their lives were growing smaller, pared down to the very basics. To move an arm independently was a wonderful achievement.

Details of Emma's first physiotherapy appointment arrived in the post and they met, in due course, with Gail, the therapist assigned to them. She would be taking Emma for a session three times a week. She shook their hands and introduced herself, her strong optimism filling the room.

'Let's get you out of this wheelchair, Emma: that's your aim, remember. It's going to be very hard, very painful, but we're going to do it.'

In the middle of every demanding exercise Gail would keep instilling the aim into her patient: 'We're going to have you walking soon, that's right . . . good girl.'

To Liz, Gail was a godsend. Until a place on the London programme materialised they were on their own. At least for now, someone else was by her side, wanting her daughter to fight against the ravages of the strokes.

At home, the wheelchair gathered dust in the hallway and Emma worked hard – she walked painstakingly to the lounge, to the bedroom, to the toilet. Liz silently thanked God for giving them the bungalow. How would they have managed to cope with stairs? The improvement was negligible, but Emma persevered.

It wasn't only Emma's body that they had to coax into action. The strokes had left her with slurred speech and her memory had also been affected.

Liz looked back through the project books charting Emma's early fight with the tumour. She pored over the pieces of lucid written work, the clever poems. She could hear her now, chattering to Jill South in the other room, full of ideas, writing rapidly. Now she sat limply in the chair, unable to even write her name. She had the use of her left hand, but it would mean starting over, learning to draw infantile letters again. And then there was her eyesight, the double vision, the blurred focus. She closed the books firmly. They had to do something.

She found Emma staring languidly out of the window.

'We're going to try writing today, in your diary.'

'But I can't, Mum. My hand doesn't work any more.'

'You still have your left hand, don't you? Try with that one.'

Emma made her first attempt. She picked up the pen awkwardly. She managed to jerk her right hand slightly to rest on the paper, holding it down, so that she could begin. Toddler-like, in huge scribbled letters, she wrote her name, covering most of the page.

'That's great. Shall I have a go now, with my left hand?'

Emma giggled at her mother's efforts. They weren't that much better than hers.

'I know, why don't we ask every visitor to write in the book using their left hand?'

'Yes. Why not? Let's make these callers work!'

Soon everyone was in on the task. Family and friends from church called in a constant stream throughout the day. Everyone would be made to write something while Emma mocked their efforts. Some played dominoes or Scrabble to keep her stimulated mentally. Her favourite game was Just a Minute. She would sit for hours with her aunt thinking of words before the egg timer ran out.

By sheer determination, she was going to recover.

One morning Emma was at her grandmother's house. Her Aunty Sue had popped in to see her and to help with lunch. Emma was sitting, bolstered on cushions, in the faded armchair in the corner of the room.

'I don't know, Emma,' said Sue, 'you will sit in my chair, and you know that's my favourite one! Are you ready for lunch yet?' Sue draped a tea towel across her niece's front to act as a bib – eating was such a messy business these days. 'I'll just go and fix the dinner.'

Ten minutes later she brought in the tray of food. Emma was singing to herself, very softly, eyes closed. Sue drew a little nearer, wondering what she was singing. Through the muffled words she could just make out the tune, then some of the words. She was singing a hymn. One of their favourite hymns:

> I am not skilled to understand
> What God has willed
> What God has planned
> I only know at his right hand,
> Stands one who is my Saviour . . .

Sue put the tray down, put her face in her hands, and cried out to God. Not once had Emma been bitter, not once bad-tempered, always trusting in her Saviour. Only God's grace could have done that.

February passed slowly, a gentle round of meals, physiotherapy, visitors and sleep. Emma made little improvement. Each day she would ask her father to write: 'felt tired today'; 'woke up feeling tired'. And so they waited for news of the London appointment.

# Chapter 14

'Happy birthday, Emma, you're looking well.'

Emma sat in her armchair as the room gradually filled. She could see the outlined faces of her family: her grandparents, Marilyn, Dyfrig, Sue, cousins, more aunties and uncles – twenty-two people had been invited in all. Her vision seemed to make the crowded room fuller. It felt as if it was bursting. So did her head. She wished she did not feel so ill, so nauseous. Her eye was infected today, on top of everything else – inflamed and angry.

Lunch was served. Her mother had laid on a sumptuous buffet: sandwiches filled with ham, egg mayonnaise and salmon; plump sausage rolls; juicy prawns spilt out of tiny vol-au-vents. Iced custard slices, Emma's all-time favourite, wobbled gently amidst the cream gateaux. Crystal glasses filled with apple and grape juice sparkled as sunshine filtered into the room. Plates filled up, people chattered.

Emma could hear herself speaking in her new slurred manner. She smiled as they sang 'Happy Birthday' and drew breath to blow out the fourteen candles on her huge cake. Fourteen years. Other girls her age would be out now with their friends, going to the cinema or to the bowling alley, and sharing pizza afterwards.

She did not say anything, of course. She joined in the merriment, laughed at her uncles' jokes. They roared over the Christmas decoration incident: 'How could Marilyn have thought it was a spider?' The cake was dissected and handed around. People came. People went. Gradually they all drifted off.

'Take care of yourself now, Emma.'

So much love; she was surrounded by love.

Her mother helped her to undress – as always, now. She pulled the useless arm out of her top for her, the useless leg out of her jeans, pushed them both into her pyjamas. She brushed her teeth for her, washed her face, and helped her into bed. Most times they laughed about the whole dressing and undressing business. Emma would say 'Can you put my shoes on, Mum?' and Liz would do just that, stuffing her feet into her daughter's shoes. She raised many eyebrows on the hospital ward doing the same thing with underwear! Tonight it did not seem so funny.

'I don't really ask why this has happened to me, Mum, but I wish that it would all go away.'

Liz hugged her close. How she wished, with every fibre of her being, that it would go away, as if it had all been a vile dream.

That night, in bed, Liz felt more memories fill in her mind. She was a thirteen-year-old girl again, watching her mother in that bed, lying dormant, unable to move. Years of bathing, feeding, dressing. She was going through it all again with her daughter.

It was not that Emma was difficult in any way. She never grumbled. She was so sweet, so brave about everything. It was just painful and frustrating to see her struggle with the simplest task. She wanted to protect Emma, to do everything for her, not watch her fumble and fall down. In the darkness as the tears came she spoke firmly to herself again: 'I must be positive. I must keep my eyes on

Jesus. I know that's the only way we're going to get through this.'

Days were so physically consuming that finding time to read the Bible was hard. Instead, Liz would bring to mind passages of Scripture. They would come back to her in the darkest of moments. She lay now, mulling over words from the book of Romans: 'If God is for us, who can be against us? . . . Who shall separate us from the love of Christ? Shall trouble or hardship? . . . No, in all these things we are more than conquerors through him who loved us . . . [nothing] will be able to separate us from the love of God that is in Christ Jesus our Lord.'[3]

And then the doubts came. The girls in work had said once: 'There's a nice God you've got, letting all those things happen to you.' Was it true? Did God hate them? Did he hate Emma? It felt like it sometimes.

She knew it wasn't true. She would just have to trust him through all of this. She felt as if she was trapped in choking blackness, trusting God with the impossible.

She hoped Emma never knew how she was feeling. Sometimes during the day she would go into their bedroom, shut the door and have a good cry, dry her eyes, and come out again. Emma never knew. Some days she would say, 'Why are you looking so sad today, Mum? I don't like to see you so sad.'

But at least she had never seen her cry.

---

[3] Romans 8:31–9.

# Chapter 15

One Friday in May, late in the afternoon, the phone rang. Pete answered it, mouthing the words 'It's the hospital' to Liz as she stood, practically on his shoulder, trying to listen. They had been waiting for this call for nearly five months. 'Yes. That should be fine. Yes. Thank you so much.' Pete replaced the receiver.

'Has she got a space, Pete?'

His eyes lit up. 'Yes. We're to take her up on Sunday afternoon. She'll have a bed on the oncology ward.'

'Who's going to tell her? She's going to be so excited.'

The one carrot dangling impossibly ahead of them now seemed within reach. They knew surgeons would never remove the tumour in Emma's head but surely the next best thing was to attack it directly with radiation. At last she had been given a chance, perhaps her last chance to put up some serious resistance to this ruinous mass in her head.

The household sprang into action. Emma sat on the bed as her mother packed her case, filling it with clothes and toiletries.

'What about train tickets, Dad?' said Emma. 'You had better do that now, before the weekend.'

Paul, his head in the newspaper, scanning the sports section, suddenly looked vaguely interested. He was taking his driving test shortly and milking every available opportunity for practice. 'I'll drive you down to the station, Dad.'

'Oh, go on then.'

Pete threw him the keys.

They drove, with typical absence of conversation, to the town. Paul had not seen his father this happy for a long time. He never voiced his feelings, but he knew the last months had been a terrible strain, watching Emma retreat from a normal child into a paralysed one. They pulled into the car park.

'You get out, Dad, and I'll park the car. I need to go into town. I'll only be ten minutes or so.'

Pete nodded with an air of resignation. He had relinquished rights to his car a long time ago. The joy of teenage sons . . .

Minutes later he emerged with the tickets. He looked around the car park. No sign of Paul. No sign of the car. He ambled around again, enjoying the sunshine. Perhaps he had missed it. The second time around, still nothing. 'He wouldn't pull a stunt today of all days, would he?' thought Pete.

Half an hour later, Paul appeared.

'Where have you moved the car, Dad?'

'I was thinking of asking you the same thing!'

Their eyes had a rare meeting. This was no practical joke – the car had been stolen! Pete felt in his pockets for loose change and they found a phone box. On the end of the line Liz was silent – another disaster to add to their growing list. 'It doesn't matter, Pete,' she said. 'We'll sort it out when we return from London. I'll ring Dyfrig now and arrange a lift for you.'

On Sunday morning the phone rang. It was the police.

'Your car has been found in Baglan Woods, Sir. We need you to pick it up.'

Pete rubbed his eyes, still crusted with sleep. It was just after seven o'clock.

'Do you mean now? I have an urgent appointment in London in a few hours time.'

'Yes, if you would, Sir.'

Outside, the early-morning air was still pregnant with dew. Where could he find transport this early on a Sunday morning? He could try Brian, maybe, his neighbour. He hesitated before pressing the tiny doorbell and shuddered at the unearthly noise it made. Brian emerged in his pyjamas with a disgruntled look on his face. As he learnt of the latest crisis, he mellowed. At least he could help with this one. 'Of course you can have the car, Pete. I'll come with you if you like. Hang on a minute.'

It didn't take long to reach the woods. They drove around for a while.

'The police said it was found in a clearing,' said Pete. 'Is that it over there?'

Brian drove them nearer. He turned the ignition off and they got out to look, their feet sliding through the wet, shimmering grass. The car had been completely stripped. Every window had been smashed. The steering wheel had been mangled. The thieves had even stolen Emma's disability badge and Christian music tapes. Pete surveyed the mess in stunned silence. 'I hope they listen to those tapes!' he said finally, with a grin. The two men chuckled as they connected the ropes, before towing the car home.

At home, arrangements had been finalised. The Sick Children's Trust, a charity providing accommodation for families outside London, had offered Pete and Liz a room in its Surgery House. They would be within the hospital grounds. They were allowed to use the house for as long as they needed, free of charge.

Paul would be staying at home while they were away. He assured them – with a wry smile – that he would keep the place in order. Various relations had been commandeered to look in on him. Liz kissed him goodbye. 'Don't have too many friends to stay. Do you promise?'

Gran and Aunty Sue came to the train station to see them off. As they got on the train Gran handed them a plastic box stuffed with rolls and home-made Welsh cakes for the journey. Emma waved until they turned the corner and leant back in her seat.

Liz stared out of the window. The train whisked through fields then towns, fields then towns. Her mind was racing. What was ahead of them? What was happening to them? Emma's illness, subsidence in the house, the car being stolen ... The twenty-third psalm, which had kept her through many dark times, came to her again:

> The Lord is my shepherd, I shall not be in want.
> He makes me lie down in green pastures,
> he leads me beside quiet waters,
> he restores my soul.
> He guides me in paths of righteousness for his
>     name's sake.
> Even though I walk through the valley of the
>     shadow of death,
> I will fear no evil,
> for you are with me;
> your rod and your staff,
> they comfort me.[4]

---

[4] Psalm 23:1–4.

A taxi dropped them outside the hospital. They stopped briefly, feeling like country mice in the wide city, as the imposing Victorian structure towered above them.

In reception they found Emma a wheelchair and asked for directions to oncology. They made their way, footsteps echoing in the narrow grey corridors. Huge windows stared down at them, paint peeling off in rivulets.

Pete pushed open the ward doors. Emma looked around. Several little children looked back. Some of them had hair, but most were bald, just pitiful little bald heads. A three-year-old girl in a cot had had both her eyes removed.

On the far end of the ward, children were screened off in isolated beds, tended to by a succession of medics in green masks and gowns. Emma was shown to her bed. Lying next to her was a young girl of nine with a strange tumour growing out of her neck.

Liz had seen similar sights to these before. To Emma it was all new. In Swansea, while having radiotherapy, she had met just one boy suffering from cancer, no other child. As they unpacked her things she looked around, finally whispering: 'Am I going to be bald again, Mum?'

By now it was dark. They left Emma to sleep and went in search of their accommodation.

The Trust house was quite homely. They had their own room. Downstairs there was a communal kitchen and lounge. It was quiet apart from the noise of the doors slamming as parents came and went. They unpacked and sat down with a cup of tea, fatigued after the journey.

A knock at the door interrupted the thoughts swarming through their brains. A hospital porter stood in the doorway, looking around.

'Are Emma's parents here?'

They looked up.

'Yes?'

'She's a little bit upset. Would you come back?'

By Emma's bed again, Liz sat stroking her forehead, soothing her to sleep. The world was frightening tonight: an unknown city, an archaic hospital, alarming sights and smells. Eventually sleep came. She gently lifted the covers over her and with hushed voices they made their way back through the eerie corridors.

# Chapter 16

On Monday morning the hospital did not seem quite so forbidding. Sun streamed into the ward, which, as it turned out, was more modern than the rest of the decrepit building. Outside they could see a pretty squared garden with benches, a meeting place for pigeons as well as patients. Emma looked at the grey brood gathering below. 'Look, that one's like me!' Sure enough, one pigeon seemed to stand out from the rest. He was a cute little creature with one badly deformed claw. He hobbled after the others, the last to reach whatever titbit they had discovered.

'Let's call him Stumpy.'

It seemed apt. He required a name if they were going to follow his antics during their stay.

The nurses drifting around the ward were very friendly. One in particular, Angela, had taken a shine to Emma. She had a mop of blonde ringlets and a face that naturally crinkled into a smile. She was engaged, soon to be married, and they discussed dresses and bouquets as she took Emma's temperature and blood pressure.

'What's happening today?' Emma asked.

'You will be meeting Mr Gilbert shortly. He's usually around mid-morning. See you later, Emma.'

At around eleven o'clock Mr Gilbert, the surgeon, swept into the ward with a pack of medical students. They did not warm to him particularly. He seemed an abrupt man. The students stood around like sheep, lamely attempting to answer the questions he barked at them. He explained loudly to his entourage what he was hoping to achieve with Emma.

'As yet, we have never been able to establish precisely what kind of tumour she has. Her surgeon in Swansea felt it was too dangerous to attempt a biopsy. I would like to try while performing the procedure. I will make an incision in the front of her head and go in deep to remove tissue. At the same time I will pass the antenna in.'

Listening from the bed they presumed the antenna was the minute tubing through which radium pellets would be passed into the tumour.

As Mr Gilbert continued Liz began to feel more and more disturbed. The operation sounded complicated as it was, but the layout of the hospital would make things even more dangerous.

'Once anaesthetised, Emma will be taken to theatre, where I will attempt to insert the tube. Still unconscious she will be taken out of theatre and across the forecourt to the scanning room where I will determine if it is in the correct place. This will happen several times before the tube is correctly positioned.'

One of the students piped up from the back: 'How long will the operation take?'

'I cannot really say at this stage – probably many hours. Afterwards she will be taken straight to intensive care. I have scheduled the operation for a week on Friday. In the meantime I will start her on a high dose of steroids, dexamethasone, in order to reduce swelling before the operation. She will also need some scans. Do you have any questions, Mr and Mrs Freeman?'

They had many, but none came out.

'Oh, and would you mind me using Emma as a case history in a lecture I am taking this week?'

They barely had time to answer before he moved on to his next patient, the students blindly following.

They were left looking at each other. Liz reassured herself. He was the best in his field. He knew what he was doing. Mr Beeston had recommended him. It was just unfortunate his manner was so poor.

Angela came by the bed and noticed their worried faces. 'Would you like to see where you'll be waking up after your operation, Emma?' she asked. It didn't sound an exciting trip, but it was better than sitting on the ward. 'I'll see if I can find a chair now. I'll be back in a minute.'

Soon they were making their way through more dark corridors to the intensive care unit. The doors swung open. Their first sight was of a famous sportsman, severely injured, sitting in a wheelchair, looking blankly towards them. If this was meant to make her feel better it was not working. 'Will I be like that?' Emma asked, looking at his motionless body.

Angela hardly noticed him. 'No. You'll be fine. Two days in here at the most.'

They took a cursory glance around the unit and left as soon as they could. Everywhere they seemed to meet horrifying sights. What were they allowing Emma to go through?

A few days later Emma sat with her parents at the front of an airy auditorium as Mr Gilbert began his lecture. She felt like a rare specimen being scrutinised and pored over. Thirty fresh-faced medical students sat staring at her, animatedly taking notes, as the surgeon expounded his theories on tumours and treatments.

At the end of the lecture Pete answered the students' questions as best he could.

'How long has she had it?'

'How did you first notice something was wrong?'

'Has she had radiotherapy?'

'What about chemotherapy?'

'How long has she been paralysed?'

The questions dried up. Mr Gilbert left. The students trickled out. They sat numbly in the empty lecture hall. Emma was worth more than this.

A visit from Paul cheered them up a little. He emerged from the coach bleary-eyed, Walkman in hand. He had been up late the previous night with friends from the street, camping in one of the back gardens, and he had slept badly.

'I rang Gran this morning to say I wasn't well and couldn't go,' he reported. 'She said, "Tough, you're going," and Grandpa put me on the coach. I'm here, but don't expect too much from me. I've got a splitting head-ache.'

Some days, Emma was allowed out for a few hours to the Trust house. Wimbledon had begun and they watched matches together in the communal lounge. She tried not to dwell on the operation looming ahead of her, but it was hard not to. There really was very little going on. Apart from taking the steroid medication and going for the scans, she had been more or less left on her own.

The following week Mr Gilbert came to see them one more time.

'I want to stress the risks of the operation with you before you sign the consent forms. There will be a con-siderable risk of Emma's vision and movement deteriorat-ing further. There will also be the usual risks that come with any operation. You have twenty-four hours to think things over before deciding finally.'

Emma jumped in quickly. 'I want to go ahead with it. I'm ready now.'

Pete could see the determination written over her face. He couldn't deny her this. He wasn't a gambling man, but if he had been, the odds of success did not seem very high at all. He signed the forms on her behalf.

The anaesthetist came by to discuss the pre-op procedure. Finding out she suffered from asthma, he instructed Emma to have four puffs of Ventolin before coming up to theatre.

'I'll see you in the morning, Emma,' he said.

# Chapter 17

At eight o'clock on Friday morning the nurse arrived to take Emma up to the pre-op room.

'I'm sure the anaesthetist told Emma to take Ventolin before we go,' Liz remarked.

'Oh, I'm not going to meddle with that,' she replied, and took hold of the wheelchair firmly.

More corridors, into the lift, and out again. The room was tiny. People were crowded in like tubes in a medicine cabinet. The anaesthetist was charming. 'Come in, Mother.'

Somehow they inched their way in. He checked Emma's name tag. 'She's had her Ventolin, yes?'

'No, she hasn't.'

He exploded. 'No? I gave strict instructions.'

He began to denigrate the nurse, who was already wilting in the crush.

'I've got Emma's inhaler with me. Would that help?' Liz offered as the tirade died down.

'Mothers, what would we do without mothers, nurse?'

'He would kiss me if there was room,' Liz thought.

'Look at your mum and start counting. When you wake up you'll be on the ward, Emma.'

As Emma dropped into unconsciousness, Liz left, tears threatening. Outside they fell, fast and heavy, choking tears. Pete paced back and forth as they waited for some news.

At half past twelve a nurse came to fetch them. Emma was out of theatre already. She could not tell them much, only that they had not been able to carry out the operation. They had attempted to insert the tubing but it had been too dangerous. 'Come up with me to intensive care,' she said. 'You can see her now.'

Emma was conscious. She looked pale. Her head was bandaged where the incision had been made but otherwise she looked normal. Liz bent to kiss her. As she did she felt Emma's right arm shaking violently against her.

'You just try and get some rest now, Emma, we'll be right here.'

And so they sat in yet another intensive care unit, willing the unforgiving minutes on.

In the opposite bed lay a nineteen-year-old girl, encased in metal wires, a solid bar holding her jaw open. She had been in a riding accident that day and her face and body had been badly crushed. Her parents were also by her side, barely speaking. Through the night she had ugly choking fits. They sat, listening, impotent in the darkness, until her rasping breath settled again.

By morning Emma seemed to have made a remarkable recovery. The professor of paediatrics came to assess her and was amazed. 'Most people are out for the count for days after an operation like this. She is quite a plucky young lady. If she carries on she can go back to the ward.' She was transferred to oncology that day.

'How did the operation go, Mum?'

'We're not sure yet. We have to wait until we see Mr Gilbert.'

'My arm is shaking a lot. Do you think it will stop soon? And my eyes – everything is a lot more blurred than usual.'

'Try not to worry, Emma. We'll be seeing the doctor soon.'

Liz had, of course, noticed her arm. Normally so limp, it seemed now to have a life of its own, swinging wildly in spasms. At lunchtime she had to hold it down so that Emma could eat.

Mr Gilbert came to see them later that day. 'The operation did not work I'm afraid,' he said, adding, 'Emma will need to continue the steroid treatment at home.' With that he went to move on.

Pete jumped in. 'Mr Gilbert, before you go. We are a little concerned about Emma's eyesight?'

'She'll just have to wear a patch.'

He tried again. 'And her arm, it hasn't stopped shaking since the operation.'

'I'm afraid there's nothing I can do about that. I did stress the risks to you.'

With that he left.

They sat together on the hospital bed. It had all gone horribly wrong. Pete struggled to find something positive to say. 'Well, at least we can go home now.'

'If the house is still standing after Paul,' Emma drawled.

The thought of the missing member of the family fired them into action.

'Pete. Perhaps you should go and find out about the discharge process?'

Back at the Trust house they packed their things hurriedly. Liz glanced at the prescription she had been given to take home with them. 'I can't understand this at all, Pete. It's still a very high dose of steroids. Mr Beeston would start reducing these by now.'

Emma had been on the tablets for two weeks. Her face was swollen, her cheeks puffy, her ankles and legs bulging.

'Let's just go home, Liz. Let's just take her home.'

The return train journey was worse. Emma felt slower, bigger. The rocking motion made her head ache, her vision blurred around her. Pete and Liz sat across from her. Outside hospital surroundings they saw with different eyes what they had not seen before. The steroids really had done some damage. She did not look like their Emma any more. Her once tiny seven-stone frame that survived on pancakes had ballooned to nearly twelve. How could they let her face everyone?

A taxi took them home from the station. They helped her out of the car. A neighbour walking past stopped to welcome them. She took one look at Emma. 'Good gracious, Emma, you've put weight on. You look as if you're pregnant. I'd never have recognised you.'

Liz felt the anger rise inside her. How could she, after all Emma had been through?

'Let's go inside, Emma.'

The neighbour stood staring as they closed the door.


The house was immaculate. Beds made, carpets vacuumed, kitchen and bathroom gleaming. They smelt a rat immediately.

'Come on Paul – how did you do it?'

They dragged the information out. When he heard they were going to be on the next train he started to sweat. The house was a disaster zone. He had phoned every friend he could think of to enlist their help.

'How much did you pay them, Paul?'

'Oh no, I didn't part with any money.'

They laughed over a cup of tea, sharing stories of the last weeks. Emma seemed no different to Paul. He did not notice her disabilities, her changing appearance. She was just his sister, just Emma.

It was good to be home, the family together again, one against the outside world. They had felt like this coming home after Emma's strokes. Only this time she had deteriorated even further.

What did the future hold for her now?

# Chapter 18

'Is there no way of getting a message to him? Yes ... I understand.'

Pete replaced the phone despondently. He had been trying to speak with Mr Gilbert for several days now, with little success. They were convinced Emma's steroid prescription was too high and yet nobody would talk to them about it. In their home on the Welsh hills the isolation was crippling.

Emma could not continue like this. Every day she woke feeling heavier, slower, more flesh adding itself to her powerless body. Purple stretch marks were appearing in thick grooves over her abdomen and legs. She had suffered several indignities during her illness but this was the worst. She had always been a beautiful child, and despite the strokes was still a charmingly pretty teenager, but now the tumour was eating into her appearance as well. Everybody was noticing her weight gain and less kindly visitors were letting her know of it. One friend came out of her room in tears, shaking his head in disbelief: 'What have they done to that poor girl?'

Liz knew if she reduced the intake incorrectly Emma might experience more bleeding. She needed proper advice, but they continued to meet a wall of silence from the hospital.

One morning she had had enough. 'I don't care if they get into trouble in London, Pete. I'm ringing Mr Beeston.' She spoke to his secretary, arranging an appointment with him for later that day.

She pushed Emma into the room. Mr Beeston was at his desk, writing. As they entered he looked up for a moment and drew breath, his pen suspended in the air. Emma sat in her chair, a pitiful ballooned figure, one arm shaking. Immediately he picked up his phone, demanding to be put through to Mr Gilbert's office. 'I don't care where he is. I want to speak to him now. Now, I tell you.'

When he finally got through the air was savage. After a few minutes he slammed the phone down angrily. 'I warned him that she reacts badly to steroids. I told him this might happen,' he muttered as he wrote out a new prescription.

They watched the outburst in amazement. They realised he had always had a soft spot for Emma, but this display of concern was deeply touching. When he had calmed himself, he spoke to them firmly.

'As you might have gathered, I have just spoken with Mr Gilbert. He has explained that the operation was a failure. I am so sorry. Nevertheless, there is no excuse for leaving her on this high dose. We will do something about it now, I promise. Our first priority is to reduce the steroids; our second is to deal with this weight gain. It's got to come off, Emma. I don't want any excuses, that you love eating chocolates, that you're premenstrual. It's got to come off. I'm going to refer you for more physiotherapy and I want you to make regular appointments to see me so that we can check on your progress.'

He did not mention the tumour and they did not ask. It seemed they had come to a dead end as far as that was

concerned. The door of treatment had shut in their faces
with a dismal thud.

They left his room with a considerable challenge.
Somehow, Emma had to lose three stones in weight
without any real ability to move, let alone exercise.
Still convalescing from the operation, she was in the
wheelchair most of the time, only managing a few
steps.

The next few months were not going to be easy.

It was a month before they received details of Emma's
physiotherapy appointments. She started sessions again
in July, with Gail, three times a week.

Gail bit her lip on seeing her patient. They had worked
so hard together a few months ago. Emma had been trying
doggedly to walk. Gail took one look at her swollen body,
her damaged arm. The goal posts had been dragged even
further away. Warmly, gently, she explained the new
programme.

'We'll be concentrating on exercising your shoulder and
arm muscles, Emma. We'll also be working on your
abdomen, hips, leg and foot. Because of the muscle loss
your body is working out of line. The movements will
attempt to compensate that.'

The sessions were extremely painful. The more Gail
pushed and stretched the limbs, the more lactic acid she
released, leaving Emma's skin blushing, raw. At times
Emma would scream with the excruciating pain; people
passing by in the corridors stealing a glance, wondering
what the noise was about.

Physiotherapy took up most of the day. A session in
the morning, lunch, rest, exercises at home, more rest. The
progress was slow and discouraging. As Emma managed
to move her arm more the tremor seemed to become even
worse. Her body mass was hindering any progress made.

They had been trying to eat healthily, but Emma had only managed to lose a few pounds. She sat one morning with a crumpled photograph of herself in her lap. 'Will you please throw this away, Mum?'

Liz felt like screaming. How she hated this tumour, the way it was slowly strangling her daughter. She sat down with her, looking her straight in the eyes. 'Now, you listen to me. You are beautiful and you always will be. This picture's not really you, Emma. I promise we will do something about your weight.'

Trawling through every recipe book she could find, Liz drew up a strict diet plan for the household. The men, needless to say, were none too pleased. That night they sat down to low-fat spaghetti bolognese. After prodding the meatless heap on his plate a few times with his fork, Paul looked at his mother.

'What's this, Mum?'

'Quorn,' she answered.

The look of disgust on his face was tangible.

Alongside the diet plan, they started a weigh-in book. Each week Liz carefully charted Emma's weight loss or gain. It was agonisingly slow. At most she lost two or three pounds a week. Most weeks she lost one pound, but the weight did come off.

By October she had dropped under eleven stone. By February she dropped to less than ten stone. The following year she would drop to less than nine stone.

Mr Beeston was delighted. 'You're doing a wonderful job, Mother,' he would gush as they went for his appointments. 'Keep up the excellent work, Emma.'

And yet all the time Emma faced setbacks. As soon as the steroids left her system, a layer of fine downy hair appeared over her face and back, closely followed by acne. Her hair started to fall out again, not completely, but enough for people to notice it was thinning. Her joints ached. Mr Beeston did not seem to offer any medication for the symptoms.

This period was the hardest of all. Emma's illness was no longer 'critical' but 'chronic'. The adrenalin of waiting for the next scan, the next operation, had been ripped from them. There were no avenues left medically. Physiotherapy would help to keep Emma more mobile, but that was all. One by one, visitors dropped off.

One morning they were in the supermarket doing the weekly shop, Emma in her wheelchair. On the way around the store Liz met two friends. 'How's Emma?' one of them whispered.

Liz could feel her hackles rise, her mother instincts smarting. Couldn't they see her? Why were they acting as if she wasn't there?

'You can ask her yourself, she's right here.'

She watched them drop their faces in embarrassment before moving on. How could they be so unthinking, so unkind? Suddenly the shop with its cloying cheery music and the bleeping tills seemed oppressive. The ceiling and the aisles started to spin. She strained to push the wheelchair out of the store as if she were pushing through sand, their faces before her, staring, sympathetic. The doors opened and she felt the cold air hit them.

In her lowest of moments she felt God really had given up on them. They went through the motions of going to church. People were kind. They prayed for Emma in the prayer meetings. The young people would visit sometimes. But in a way it made everything more painful. Emma was fifteen now. She should be like them.

Life should be opening out before her, not closing down.

# Chapter 19

Towards the end of September Mr Fish paid another visit. Emma had missed almost an entire year of schooling since December and the first stroke. He felt it was time she started to pick up on her studies.

'Will I have Jill South again?'

'No, I've got someone else in mind, Emma, someone I think is going to be just right for you.'

A week later in walked a tall, grey-haired lady, a polished leather handbag fixed to her elbow. 'Hello, you must be Emma,' she remarked in a stern, clipped voice, before setting out her plans. Emma warmed to the formidable Mrs B. A. Leyshon instantly.

She came each day for an hour, and as Emma felt stronger this increased to two hours, setting a piece of homework before she left. Together they covered the work she would have been doing in school.

Every morning, as they stopped for coffee, Emma plagued her repeatedly. 'Go on, tell me your other name!'

Eventually, she announced, 'It's Arathusa, Emma, Arathusa.'

Her full title, Beryl Arathusa Leyshon, appeared on every piece of correspondence and homework after that.

By the time autumn drifted in, days were starting to become pleasantly full – tutoring in the morning, physiotherapy in the afternoons. Emma started to walk a little more in the house, although she needed the wheelchair when they went out. They discovered an easy walk along the Mumbles coast where they could push the chair. Emma would manage a few yards at a time on someone's arm, taking in the blustery sea air, watching the boats huddling together, moored for the winter.

Family were her main companions. Her grandparents and aunts accompanied her on trips out or popped in for coffee. She had very few friends her own age. Girlfriends visited only occasionally now, intimidated by the illness that had taken hold of her. In a way it was easier. Being around girls her own age only served to remind her of the life she was missing out on, of how obscure she seemed to be.

One night that winter two girls from the street called to see her on their way out to a party. Emma sat in her chair looking at their miniskirts and strapless tops, their cheeks smeared with luminous makeup. Think of something to say, some funny line . . .

'Where are your coats?' she blurted out.

'Oh, you can't take coats to the disco, Emma.'

Of course not, stupid thing to say. I sound like my mum, stupid thing to say. She sat wishing they would go away. Wishing she could cry.

She was most at ease with her brother and his friends. On Saturdays they would congregate to watch some big sporting event. Sometimes there would be nine strapping lads draped over the floor. Emma would perch in the middle of them, listening to their shouting, giggling as they placed orders for food with 'Bet' and 'Dave', their names for the aged parents.

As the following year opened she began to study for her GCSEs. She was taking six: Maths, English Language,

English Literature, Child Development, Catering, and Office Practice. The subjects were not her first choice. Before the stroke had affected her eyesight and memory she had shown a flair for languages. Now she had to choose subjects she could cope with.

As the exam dates drew nearer Mr Fish came to assess her. Because of the double vision, reading was laborious. Emma was still writing with her left hand, her right hand shaking badly, and her handwriting was poor. He decided the best method would be for her tutor to read out the questions and for Emma to dictate the answers to her. She would be allowed extra time and he would bring in an adjudicator to ensure exam conditions were met.

Pete and Liz recorded her notes on a Dictaphone and Emma played them monotonously in her bedroom for weeks leading up to the exams.

In June the papers arrived in official envelopes. Emma sat at the dining room table looking at the blurred image of Mrs Leyshon as she read out the first question. She thought of her friends now. They would be sitting this one too, in muted schoolrooms, pens at the ready, making faces at each other across the crowded desks, comparing answers afterwards. Concentrate, Emma. Concentrate. She racked her brain for the answers. 'Quadratic equations . . . '

'I've got your results, Emma. Would you like me to open them?'

She had passed them all. Mrs Leyshon beamed at her pupil. She had done so well. She had been an absolute pleasure to teach.

Emma handed her a present as a thank you. 'We've spent a long time looking for this.'

From inside the coloured wrapping a sack-like handbag emerged, coloured in thick stripes of mud brown and fungal green. They had scoured second-hand shops to find one revolting enough for their joke.

'It's . . . er . . . very nice,' she smiled politely.

Emma guffawed. 'That's not your real present. Look underneath the tissue paper!'

Afterwards, as Mrs Leyshon hugged Emma goodbye and got into her car, she called back, 'By the way, it's not Arathusa, it never was, you know – just plain Anthea.'

And she drove off with a wave, like the Queen.

# Chapter 20

One morning, at the end of their session, Gail took Liz to one side.

'I seem to have reached a plateau, Liz. We're not making any real progress now. She might benefit from additional therapy. I know of someone who might be able to help. You would have to fund the treatment yourself, but I'm sure it would be worth it.'

Even the ever-positive Gail had reached the end of the line. She wrote down a number for Liz. Irene, a therapist who specialised in neurological cases, ran a private practice in Merseyside.

Liz got in touch as soon as they were home. Irene's voice came through on the other end of the line.

'How old is she? What kind of accident was it?'

'She has a brain tumour. She's had a shunt inserted, a catheter, radiotherapy, two strokes. The last operation has made her deteriorate further. She can hardly walk and only has the use of one arm.'

Liz listened to herself detailing the last six years of her daughter's life, the catalogue of her sufferings condensed into single brutal sentences.

Irene seemed very positive.

'I've been working with a young woman who couldn't walk after a car accident. She was determined to walk down the aisle on her wedding day and last week I saw her do just that. I'm sure we'll be able to do something for Emma.'

They had not been given hope for some time now. This was like taking a great big gulp of fresh air. Liz booked Emma in for an intensive course. They would make a holiday out of it, along with Pete's parents, and stay in a neighbouring hotel. The sessions would take place in the mornings, leaving afternoons free.

They turned up for the first morning session, absorbing the sight of yet another therapy building. Irene introduced herself. She was a dark-haired young woman, very trim, kitted out in sweatpants and shirt. Emma sensed she would be in for some hard work.

As they began Irene handed Liz a video camera. Liz looked at it nervously. 'What's this for?'

'I want you to video all the exercises I'm doing with Emma. You'll be able to play them back at home and copy them.'

'Oh, all right then.'

Liz's mind flashed back to the radiotherapy room. She had taken all those photographs of Emma, lying on her front, her skin marked up in preparation for the toxic rays. Here she was again, videoing her daughter's struggles to move her limbs. She shook herself back to the present.

'Which button do I press?'

Irene worked Emma relentlessly. The first exercises involved lifting her paralysed arm up and down, then sideways, simultaneously stretching and massaging the dead muscles. Emma was still quite heavy, still quite immobile. After ten minutes she was panting like a woman in labour, translucent with sweat.

Irene helped her to manipulate her 'dead' right hand by using her left hand to flatten it out, to hold a piece of paper down, or clasp it to hold a pen.

'Don't be afraid of it, Emma.'

Movements once so spontaneous now made her wince in agony. In one exercise, her hands clumsily clapping over her head, she bore considerable resemblance to a sea lion! She sat good-humouredly as the two women around her expressed their amusement.

At the end of the week she leant back on Irene, exhausted.

'Thank you so much.'

'It's been a privilege, Emma, you've worked so hard. You're a lovely girl.'

The week had been a success. Emma had made real progress. Her balance had improved and her arm was more mobile. She would continue to make progress as they went through the exercises at home.

Liz put the tape in the machine. They would begin that morning. She looked again at the image on the screen: Emma's face, straining with every ounce of energy she could summon, blushing as they laughed at her sea lion exercise. She was always so positive, always trying. Not once during the week had she ever been bad-tempered, not once discouraged or self-pitying.

The tape continued playing. Liz could see her daughter's clumsy body.

What shone through so strongly was her sweet temperament in suffering.

# Chapter 21

The summer holidays meandered to a close, only this time there would be no new school year for Emma. Her exams completed, she had finished home schooling. Physiotherapy sessions with Gail had run their course. Hospital appointments were now merely annual check-ups. Mr Beeston, her great friend and ally, was in semi-retirement. The main strands of her life had been evacuated with nothing to replace them. Nobody actually said it but everybody was feeling it. What was Emma going to do with herself now?

Physically it seemed she had recovered as much as she was ever going to. She could walk short distances, dragging her paralysed leg, falling from one side to another. She felt moderately well but too much activity caused exhaustion and headaches. She relied heavily on her parents. She needed help to take a bath, although she could now dress on her own. She could potter around the house but did not have the stamina or balance to cope with basic domestic tasks. Her days were long. She could only read for short periods because of her vision. There was nothing for her to do.

Pete's boss in work, Eric Sallis, noticed his unusually low spirits one morning.

'What's up, Pete?'

'Oh, just Emma. We're finding things difficult at the moment.'

'Have you tried the Christian Lewis Trust?'

'No?'

'It's a Trust to help families affected by cancer. They might be able to help in some way.'

Pete returned to the growing pile of paperwork on his desk. If they could just put Emma in touch with other teenagers in similar situations it would be something. As it was, she felt so alone.

At home he dialled the number. He got through to Judith May, the Trust's care officer. She seemed friendly. He related Emma's story to her.

'You mean the tumour was diagnosed when she was nine and she's fifteen now?' asked Judith. There was a mortified silence. 'Hospitals usually contact us when they have a child with cancer, but we have never received her details. She must have slipped through the net.'

'We never use the word cancer: they've never proved the tumour is malignant.'

'I am so sorry. I'm sure we can be of some help to Emma.'

Pete put the phone down feeling a little more positive.

They met up with Judith and the other helpers the following week at the Trust headquarters. They were kind people. The Trust had been set up in memory of a little boy, Christian Lewis, who had lost his battle with cancer in 1983.

Judith shook Emma's hand warmly. 'How are you coping, Emma?'

Judith looked puzzled at the straight reply: 'Oh, I'm fine. God's looking after me.'

A volunteer gave Emma a brief tour of the office. In every room photographs of smiling children were crammed on to pin boards. Emma scanned them in detail. Hundreds of lives touched by all kinds of tumours, just like the tumour in her head. Some of the faces had the familiar swollen look, many wore baseball caps. For a moment she didn't feel quite so obscure, quite so alone.

Privately, Judith suggested to Liz and Pete that they might like to attend one of the Trust's support groups. There was a meeting that week. Everything would be quite informal. It was simply an opportunity to meet and chat with other parents in similar situations. They looked at each other. They had been alone for years in their suffering – it seemed strange to start talking about it now. Somewhat reluctantly, they agreed to go along.

Inside the room they helped themselves to coffee, made their introductions and sat down on the plastic chairs. They listened quietly as parents in the thick of a child's suffering started, one by one, to recount their individual stories. Some had only just been diagnosed. Others were in the middle of debilitating treatments, struggling to cope with hair loss, sickness. Some confessed to problems with brothers and sisters in the family: 'They feel so ignored'; 'He's starting to have violent tantrums.' Others revealed the tension in their marriages. Emotions were palpable across the room.

Each month people dropped out. They did not discuss the departures. A separate support group existed for bereaved parents. Sometimes one parent would stop coming, tensions in the marriage finally coming to a head.

Some nights there would be discussion on alternative therapies – transcendental mediation, diets, yoga, reflexology. They never went to those.

Liz and Pete felt more and more alienated, abstracted on every level. It wasn't that they hadn't experienced some of these emotions, just that they had done so years before.

These parents still had hope: they were still living for the next scan, the next round of treatment.

One evening, when it was their turn, Pete spoke. He told Emma's story up to the present. 'Medically, doctors can do little else for her. She should really have died and yet she hasn't.'

'How do you cope with that kind of pressure, with the "unknown" hanging over you?'

'We just do, day by day, trusting in God.'

No one there was in the same place as them. Their family seemed to have grown stronger and closer since that sickening day of the first scan. Why was that? They were not better people, any more moral, any more courageous, and yet they felt so different from those around them.

Deep within, they knew why. God had made the difference. He had kept them as a family in the years since Emma's diagnosis. Christians over Swansea, indeed over the world, their friends in Sweden and Germany – all had prayed for them. They were seeing now the value of those prayers. Without them they could so easily have split up as a couple. Paul could have reacted badly to the attention Emma received. Emma could have retreated into a bitter shell. God had been so faithful to them.

The support group in time came to a natural end. It had helped. They had seen that for all those moments of aloneness God had been with them all the time.

In the meantime Emma was enjoying visits to Judith at the office. Once or twice a week Liz would drop her off and she would help out with filing or answering the phone. It served to bring some routine to her empty days and gave her a degree of independence.

One particular day Emma happened to mention that she was a big fan of a certain children's television presenter. Her sixteenth birthday was approaching and Judith had been looking out for an idea for a birthday treat. They had offered to arrange a trip to Disneyland but Emma had refused to go – she didn't want any fuss. At least now Judith had something to work on.

A few weeks later Judith presented Emma with an envelope. Inside were four tickets to see the musical *Grease*, in which the teen idol was starring. The hotel had been booked and the train tickets reserved. They simply had to turn up. Emma was thrilled. She asked an old school friend, Nicola Dyer, if she would like to be her guest, and that Saturday they left with her parents for London.

From beginning to end they were given VIP treatment. At Paddington a cab pulled up for them. The driver, Jimmy, was their chaperone for the day. The first stop was the hotel to freshen up. 'I'll pick you up in an hour,' said Jimmy, and pulled up again to take them on a tour of the capital. 'I'll be back after your evening meal to drive you to the theatre' he said as he dropped them back at the hotel. The girls were in their element. They had a personal chauffeur!

The hotel was quite grand. In their rooms they giggled and dressed excitedly in their evening outfits. Emma caught a glimpse of herself in the tall mirror. She had slimmed down now to her correct weight and looked quite glamorous. Her hair, still thin, was cut to a short bob and not as noticeable. Contact lenses disguised the oversized pupil in her eye. If she held her arm firmly to stop it shaking, she looked normal. Liz looked at her as she came from the room. 'You look beautiful, Emma, beautiful.'

Jimmy drove them to the Dominion Theatre. Once inside they were shown to their seats by the manager. 'I've arranged for Emma to come backstage at the end of the performance. Don't tell her anything,' he whispered to Liz as the lights receded.

At the end of the show Emma felt a presence by her shoulder. 'Emma. Would you like to follow me backstage?'

The star was waiting to meet her in his dressing room. 'Come in, Emma, I'm not going to bite you. Give me a kiss then!'

Liz rummaged in her bag for the camera, tissues and sweets falling to the floor as she tried frantically to insert a film.

'Oh, these Welsh with their cameras!'

Outside, Jimmy was waiting for them again, this time to take them to Planet Hollywood. They walked past scores of people squashed in the queues straight to the front, where the manager was again waiting for them. Nicola spent the entire evening with her mouth open.

They returned to the hotel at midnight feeling thoroughly spoilt.

# Chapter 22

At home life was monotonous and dull again. Emma
needed more than a morning's voluntary work at the Trust
to occupy her days. Liz made an appointment for her with
the careers officer at the local job centre.

They sat in front of a desk. A woman stared inquisitively
at them, a wad of forms waiting to be filled at her side.
She had seen the young girl hanging on to her mother's
arm. They knew what she was thinking.

'Can you walk unaided?'

'Well, short distances.'

She looked at Emma's arm moving wildly.

'Can you write?'

'I can type. I have six GCSEs.'

She scanned the computer screen quickly.

'It's going to be difficult to find a suitable job for you
. . . with such . . . limited physical ability.'

Liz wanted to yell at her, 'Did you know my daughter
was one of the brightest in her class before her stroke?
Did you know she excelled at sports and languages and
literature?' Instead, she sat politely, trying to ignore the
woman's patronising comments.

'Oh, there is something that might be suitable. One of
the hospitals is taking on young people with disabilities
in the records department. You would work up to sixteen
hours a week without affecting your disability benefit in

any way. Would you like application forms? You know how to get there?'

They nodded – they knew how to get there.

Emma left the job centre feeling optimistic. This seemed ideal. She would surely be able to manage sixteen hours a week sorting notes, filing, typing into a computer. She would be meeting people, escaping the house, widening her world a little.

After an interview and medical she heard she had been successful. She would work half days and build up her hours as she felt able. She would be starting with Kate, a hearing-impaired girl she had met on her interview. They would be new girls together.

On her first day she woke earlier than usual and dressed in the smart outfit they had picked out the night before. Liz dropped her outside the hospital. 'It's just through those doors, Emma. It's not far. Have a good morning.'

Liz watched her stumble over the uneven path and felt herself move to help her. She stopped herself – she had to let her go now. In the car on the way home she prayed: 'Please Lord, let it go well. She needs this so much. Please be with her.'

At lunchtime Liz was in the hospital car park, waiting. She saw Emma standing outside dejectedly and walked over to meet her.

'How did it go?'

'It was awful, Mum. I couldn't do anything. I couldn't carry the notes. My arm was shaking so badly, everything kept falling. I felt so clumsy. They gave me some names to type into the computer but after minutes my head was thundering and the screen a blur. In the end I just sat there.'

Liz felt Emma lean heavily on her arm. She was shaking more. She didn't have the energy to let herself into the car. Liz tried to make light of it. 'It'll get better. Everyone feels out of their depth on their first day.'

At home Emma lay on the sofa. Her head ached. It had not ached like this for ages. Perhaps after a good night's sleep . . .

She persevered for three weeks. She would spend the mornings feeling incompetent, unable to carry out the simple tasks given to her. Kate had settled into the job well and she felt useless in comparison. She would spend the afternoons with appalling headaches, lying around the house. Her energy levels sapped to nothing. She required help to dress, help to walk into work.

All the time Pete and Liz were looking on, wondering if the additional pressure would bring on another bleed, another stroke, devouring what was left of her weakening muscles.

Eventually Liz suggested that she hand in her resignation. It seemed to be a defeating exercise on all fronts.

'We'll look for something else, Emma. I promise.'

In the job centre again, the woman perused the same lists on her screen.

'Well, there is a computer training scheme running over three weeks.'

'I'll give it a try. I'll try anything.'

Liz deposited Emma outside the building, knowing the outcome. It was computer-based work – there would be the same problem. Sure enough, at the end of the day, there she was looking miserable.

'It's the screens, Mum. After minutes I can feel my headache starting up.'

'Never mind, we'll find something else. There must be something out there for you.'

But there just did not seem to be anything. Clerical work was not an option as it aggravated Emma's headaches.

Physical activity of any kind caused exhaustion. Pete tentatively asked if she would like to look at a day centre for disabled adults.

'I'll give it a try, Dad. You'll come with me, though, won't you?'

That morning they drove up to the centre. Pete helped Emma out of the car, steadying her as they made their way to the entrance. Emma gaped inside. The room was packed. People, mostly old, were sitting around in worn armchairs, some playing dominoes, most sitting, staring emptily into space. A thick wave of cigarette smoke hit her. They were all profoundly mentally and physically disabled. In the middle of the room sat a huge dog, saliva dribbling down his jowls.

That was it. She couldn't even go inside. She knew the reaction she had to animal fur would be too severe. She had suffered from the allergy since a tiny child. It had never really bothered her, and today she was glad she had it – glad that huge dog sat in the choking room.

She knew she was disabled. She just did not feel ready to be *that* disabled. Anyhow, this seemed to be the wrong place for her entirely. She was young. She was mentally astute. The stroke had not affected her that way, at least.

Depression set in for the first time with an iron hold. There was nothing for her to do. What did she exist for? What was her purpose? She knew God had spared her life, but for what? A day a week working in a cancer charity? Was that it?

Life choices seemed like a row of skittles knocked down cruelly, one by one, in front of her. She couldn't work. She wasn't meeting up with people her own age anywhere, let alone members of the opposite sex. The last time she dated a boy had been at her tenth birthday party, just before the tumour had reared its ugly head again. She wondered if she would ever marry. Doctors had stressed her body would not cope with the rigours of pregnancy and childbirth. Who would want her anyway?

Day after day she woke numbly, dressed, and sat in the lounge, her body shaking, unable to read or write much, watching the television intermittently, mulling over the last years in her mind.

This room had witnessed everything. She had lain here exhausted from the radiation and vomiting. She had hidden here from the world with her bald skull. She had struggled to walk here, learnt to hold a pen again, tried to lose that weight, struggled through exams, looking on through the window at friends in the street, playing, growing up, and moving away.

Somebody was with her every minute of the day, assisting with the smallest task. When her father worked, her mother stayed with her. When her mother worked, her father looked after her. Her grandparents and aunties invited her to their homes in between. Paul was at university now. So much for independence . . .

And then there was the tumour, that rotting orange in her head. What if it bled again? What if she had another, further, paralysing stroke? What if that headache for the hundredth time that day meant something more ominous? She felt trapped enough in her body as it was without the threat of further deterioration. Constantly, the tumour was there, inside her, growing invisibly, insidiously, making the frail life she possessed even more insecure.

Night after night she got into bed, pulled the covers over her, wondering if this was her last, wondering if she might never wake up again.

Slowly, deliberately, the depression consumed her. It came out first of all in panic attacks. They would strike mostly in the middle of the night. She would wake in a cold sweat, her heart racing, her mind playing macabre tricks: what if she did some harm to herself or to her parents? Fumbling in the darkness she found the door handle, found the door to her parents' room and stood in the velvet darkness crying helplessly.

Evenings became a phobic ritual. She hid behind her parents, making them check the locks on every window, every door, sometimes several times, in case someone broke in to harm them in the night.

By day she became anxious and withdrawn, afraid to go outside. Repeatedly she would ask if her parents loved her, over and over again, staring at them with big wondering eyes. If she slipped, dropped something, said the wrong thing, it would drive her to despair.

'I'm sorry. You do forgive me, don't you?'

They appeared again, the same childlike, wondering eyes.

Pete and Liz looked on, impotent. This was not the Emma they knew. She had always had such a sunny disposition – nothing would defeat her. They felt powerless again in this new phase of her suffering: reassurance, talking, comforting – nothing worked. Slowly, their sixteen-year-old daughter was retreating into herself, like an insect into its dark cocoon.

Pete knew what she was feeling, of course. He felt it himself. Medically she should not really be here. She was living on borrowed time. A consultant had once told him that if five years passed 'it was a good sign'. Emma's tumour had made its presence known in her ninth year. Five years later, in her fourteenth year, it had reared its head again by bleeding, causing the two mutilating strokes. Five years on, she would be nineteen. Three years of waiting to clear the next psychological barrier.

If he was honest, he always expected the worst. If she complained of a headache, mentally he was in the car, racing down the motorway behind the ambulance. If he felt that way, no wonder she was going through it.

Two whole years passed in much the same way.

# Chapter 23

Eventually, in sheer desperation, Pete asked Emma if she would try some counselling. He knew a trained Christian counsellor who had offered to help.

Emma agreed and went several times to talk with her at a local counselling centre. She was a well-meaning lady, but the sessions did not help. They talked around the problem for an hour. At home Emma would think around the problem again. The problem never went away. Her tumour was not going anywhere; her disabilities were permanent.

The years of her courageous faith and trust in God seemed to have evaporated. The night of the Luis Palau campaign, before the strokes had invaded her sleeping body, was now a pale insipid memory. Church was no longer a joy – it hadn't been for some time. Preaching did not affect her in any way. Apart from her family, she had few Christian friends.

She certainly did not feel part of the church's young people's group. Every meeting they arranged was out of her remit, yet another activity she could not join in with – swimming, or bowling, or walking. She would return from the meetings wallowing in another bout of self-pity.

'I just hate watching everybody having fun. I'm on the outside all the time, looking in.'

'It's not their fault, Emma. They don't mean to exclude you. They're just normal young people.'

'Exactly, and I'm not normal.'

Pete was also going through it. For years now there had been divisions in the church and, as an elder, he bore the weight of the problems, returning heavily from yet another bitter meeting. Eventually he decided to resign – they would leave and look for another church.

Inside, Liz felt as if she had reached breaking point. How much more could they take as a family? The one place they should have found comfort was only a source of more grief. Were they wrong over the divisions in the church? Were they wrong to leave? So many Christians had prayed for them as a family over the years. What would they think of them now?

In the middle of the troubled period a friend asked if Emma would accompany her to a leading church in the city. It was lively, charismatic worship. She might enjoy it. Emma, typically open, went along.

It was certainly different. The church was full to capacity, the singing loud, rhythmic. She thought she might give it a try for a while.

One Sunday morning she sat in the crowd listening to a visiting preacher, half concentrating as usual. Nothing much from the Bible seemed to move her these days. Most of the time she felt God had given up on her.

Suddenly she sat up and took note. The preacher was asking if anybody there wanted to be healed. '"Does anybody want to be healed?" I want to be healed,' she thought.

Amazingly she had never really considered it before. She had wished in a dream-like way that the tumour was not there and she could be normal. But this was different. Here was somebody asking her if she actively wanted to be healed. She lived resigned to the fact that she would not be; that she was really dying.

The preacher continued. 'Can you imagine that God, who has dealt with your sin, cannot deal with your sicknesses?'

Her mind was alert now, her heart racing. She had never thought of it this way.

Years earlier, when she was nine, people had had faith then. Her mother had laid hands on her in that hospital bed, and later the minister of the church had done the same. The elders had anointed her with oil, praying the prayer of faith. But nothing had happened and gradually any thoughts of healing had faded. Her healing had been survival, but survival for what? What kind of life was this?

'Yes. I want to be healed!'

She felt like shouting it aloud, to the four corners of the auditorium.

The preacher was telling the congregation now of those he had seen healed. As he gave each example, people around her were shouting and cheering, even applauding. He was insistent. 'If you believe in God, come to the front. We know that he's going to heal today. I can sense his power working. Just come. Make your way to the front.'

In the background the band was playing, quietly at first, then louder, until she could hardly hear herself think over the heavy base beat.

The congregation was impassioned, frenzied, the atmosphere charged with anticipation. Perhaps this was what it felt like to know God's spirit moving.

She got up flimsily, making her way to the platform at the front. She was trembling. It was finally going to happen. Now was her moment.

The preacher came towards her. He placed his hand on her forehead. She felt him push her, firmly, hard. So hard she fell backwards. She felt herself falling into some person's arms. They lowered her to the floor. She hurt a bit. The carpeted floor felt like granite. She lay still, her eyes closed, waiting. Perhaps this was part of the healing. She felt her arm shake. Nothing had happened yet.

Keep waiting, Emma.

Still nothing happened.

The preacher was saying something again. 'I know that God has healed in this place today. I can sense that bodies have been touched. Let's praise God together.'

The musicians struck up another song.

She felt sick to the core of her being. God had worked, but not on her. Perhaps she had not believed enough.

The person helped her to her feet. He did not say anything. The preacher had not even looked at her, not even asked how she was.

Limping, shaking, and knowing the tumour was still there, she made her way back to her seat.

As they sang the final hymn, she felt numb. Perhaps she had to keep going forward again and again until she was healed. Perhaps that was it.

At home Pete was incensed. How dare somebody push her over like that in the name of Christianity! How dare somebody taunt his daughter with the idea that if she had enough faith she would be healed! Continually they were forced to swallow this false teaching on suffering. He had been given a book recently declaring 'all illness' was a result of 'sin'. Appalled, he had thrown it across the room.

Why did Christians feel the need to place the blame for sickness at someone's door? It was their fault as parents. It was Emma's fault for not believing. And why the emphasis that life is only valuable when healing has occurred, as if Emma's life would suddenly 'begin' if the tumour was miraculously removed?

Surely the Bible taught that God had a plan for the Christian in the throes of suffering, in the middle of pain. After all, God created the blind, the deaf, the mute. He had created Emma with the tumour, as a foetus in Liz's womb. It was impossible to understand, to fathom out, but that was clearly the teaching of the Bible.

Her sickness was for a purpose. They had yet to discover that purpose, but they knew she had one. Yes, God did heal. Of course he could and did, but not at the whim of some preacher pushing desperate people to the floor. It made him mad.

Pete sat with Emma, trying to pick up the pieces, destroying the spurious hope that had been taunted in her face. She in all probability would not be healed in this life. Yes, in the next she would have a perfect body, she would be able to run and jump, she would be free from pain, her mind would soar to its limits. But unless God supernaturally intervened in his own way she would always have this tumour.

He wondered where that preacher was now. He wondered if he even cared.

# Chapter 24

After months of searching Pete and Liz settled on a church a few miles from their home. The congregation met in a stone chapel, its pewter-blue walls caking with damp. The minister, a son of the Addis manager who had prayed for Liz all those years ago, preached simply through the Bible, and the people were warm, friendly. It was good to listen to expository teaching again after the last difficult months and years, and they soaked it up. They had a found a new spiritual home.

Emma continued to attend the city church, secretly hoping, despite all her father had said, that he was wrong – the next service really was the one she would be healed in.

One Sunday night, not having a lift, she went resentfully with her parents. She sat at the back, in one of the heavy wooden pews, digesting the activity around her as people took their seats. Five minutes before the service began the heavy doors creaked open and a troop of children ran in. They filtered noisily into the front rows: teenage girls, blonde hair glinting with clips and slides; eight-year-old boys, fresh from playing in the streets, trainers thick with mud, hair dishevelled; and a toddler, carrying a bottle with a grubby hand, swept along by an older sister. Younger men got up and squeezed into any gaps they could find among them.

The service started. It was quite ordinary: songs, hymns, prayer, a Bible reading, a sermon. The children wriggled a bit. Every now and then they were squashed back into place by one of the men, or retrieved from the aisle. The toddler fell asleep, snoring thickly. Most listened, Bibles open, hands on chins to the message. At the end they charged at full speed into the back room to fight for drinks and bars of chocolate.

Emma gathered up her things, wondering if her parents would be long.

'You must be Emma. Hi, I'm Lynsey.'

A dark-haired girl was standing over her. Half an hour later they had moved into the back room, still chatting. Lynsey was the same age as her, quite shy, and they bonded naturally.

'The minibus is ready,' someone shouted and the children disappeared through the narrow back door, a trail of wrappers and polystyrene cups in their wake.

As Emma was leaving with her parents the minister introduced himself.

'This isn't my church. I go somewhere else,' she fired at him.

The following Sunday night she came back – and the next.


As the weeks passed Emma became aware of a gradual change in her mindset. She had been going to church to be healed, but now she found herself drawn because she wanted to hear the Bible explained. Somehow, out of nowhere, God was speaking to her.

Memories of that cold June day came seeping back. The vivid assurance that Jesus had died for her, given her eternal life, became real again. The Argentinian preacher then had a simple text. It was the same message here and people of all ages were discovering that lives could be changed through Jesus Christ.

She started to take along a notebook and sat fixed, concentrated, scrawling points down from the sermon in long spindly handwriting. And she took along the Bible that had been sitting so idly on her desk. Every Sunday she scrambled through its pages, her clumsy arm shaking, often dropping it on the floor, to find passages from Leviticus or Ezekiel, Mark's Gospel or Ephesians. Wherever she turned, to the Old Testament or the New, there was a truth uncovered for her, a new glimmer of light into her suppressed world.

As for her disabilities, she would sit for most of the time, and so there was little to distinguish her from everyone else. In fact, hardly anybody knew her history, the sad tale of the orange in her head. There was a sense of release in that, as if she had been given a fresh start. She didn't have to contend with sympathy, the well-meaning sidelong glances – 'Just think what she would have been doing now, poor girl.' There certainly was no pressure to be healed.

This was a work she could be a part of. She could quite easily chat to the little boy who loitered behind the others; she could sit with the restless girl who wanted to listen but so quickly became distracted. Her old sense of humour and her easy sociableness returned. She began to forge new friendships outside the constricted world she had inhabited for years.

Alongside the Bible, she rediscovered Christian books, persevering this time, a few pages a day, before the headaches won over. She consumed Joni Eareckson's writings – the American teenager paralysed from the neck down in a diving accident.

One night she was lying in bed, the lamp on, her arm shaking, throwing resonating shadows on the wall, when she came across a paragraph that made her catch breath.

> God knew that I had hands and feet and arms and legs that did not work. He knew what I looked like. And none of these things really mattered. What counted was that I was His workmanship created in His image. And He wasn't finished with me ... Not only was there purpose to my life at this point, but there was an iceberg of potential as well ... an entire new area of my life and personality not even developed yet!'[5]

So she, Emma Freeman, wasn't yet finished with. God was *working in her* to create something of great beauty and significance. A thousand thoughts started to awaken in her mind. What was it he wanted to use this frail body for? Maybe it was to pray? She had almost forgotten about prayer. She prayed every day to be healed, but only for that. What about prayer for the work of the Gospel, prayer for unbelievers? She had unlimited time on her own to use up. She could use it to speak to God. In doing that, she could do far more than with the use of all her limbs ...

Yet with every thought that God might use her plenty more came that he wouldn't. She was still plagued by insecurities. Did people really love her? Did God really love her? Had she committed some great sin for him to cause this tumour to grow in the centre of her brain?

At the end of a Bible study, in the minister's home, she ventured her question: 'Am I ill because of my sin?'

---

[5] Joni Eareckson, *Joni* (Basingstoke: Pickering & Inglis, 1984), p. 120.

People were getting up, yawning, digging around for the best biscuits on the plates being brought in from the kitchen. Pete and Liz had told him a little about her illness and her desire to be healed. He opened a Bible to 1 Peter and read a verse: 'do not be surprised at the painful trial you are suffering, as though something strange were happening to you. But rejoice that you participate in the sufferings of Christ, so that you may be overjoyed when his glory is revealed.'[6]

'Your suffering isn't God's punishment, Emma,' he said. It's his great purpose for you, to identify with Christ. Through your life, God will speak to people. Your illness will bring glory to him.'

She was unconvinced. She was sure sickness was connected with sin. The conversation shifted to other matters, coffee was handed round, and she let the subject slide.

A few months later, the church was putting on an outreach evening. A meal would be served and afterwards a short Gospel message preached. Everyone was asked to invite friends and members of their family – ones and twos came usually.

Emma listened to details of the evening. This was something she could do. She knew so many people. Her family, who had been there for her all these years, not all of them believed in Jesus. It was an opportunity for them to hear about her Saviour, to enable them to understand the hope she had. That week the phone was buzzing as one by one she invited everyone she could think of.

On the night she went into the back room of the church and reserved three tables for her guests. Over twenty members of her family came. She sat with them, falteringly

---

[6]  1 Peter 4:12–13.

eating her food, cut into manageable pieces by her mother. Usually she would be deeply embarrassed, but not tonight. She was aware that something very special was happening, as though God had, for one night, drawn back the covering of her life, giving a snap glimpse of his intentions for Emma Freeman.

Before the message, she shuffled nervously to the front of the room, putting her notes on the lectern. She had been asked to say how she had come to believe in Jesus and she was determined to go through with it.

Her arm would always shake but at that moment her whole body shook. She read out her notes, word for word: discovering the tumour, the Luis Palau meeting, the strokes.

Those listening were stunned at the young girl, at the remorseless sufferings her body had undergone. Her light voice hit into the silence that settled over the room.

At the end she said this. 'You're probably thinking to yourself right now, "Oh, bless her, hasn't she been through a lot," but it's nothing to compare with what Jesus has been through for you and me, how he suffered and died on the Cross for our sins so we can be forgiven.

'I would rather be like I am today and be a Christian than not have Jesus Christ in my life. I could say a lot more, but I just want to emphasise that God is there for us every day, helping and encouraging us.

'My doctors didn't think I would live past my early teens but God had other plans for my life. With his love I can face every day.'

She ended with her favourite verse from 1 Peter: 'Cast all your anxiety on him because he cares for you.'[7]

---

[7] 1 Peter 5:7.

Emma took her seat, trembling. The minister began his message. Her family, manly uncles with tears glistening in their eyes, sat listening to the message that she so sincerely believed. They were all there because Emma had asked them, because of the sheer weight of the life she had lived in front of them. Everyone who met her during her illness, the early years of operations and radiotherapy, the later years of the strokes, knew there was a God – she had told most people directly. How else could they explain her sweetness, her uncomplaining nature in unbearable circumstances?

Emma hugged the last relative goodbye. In the back room trestle tables were being dismantled and food remains poured into black bags. Someone had switched on the vacuum cleaner. She leant against the wall with deep satisfaction.

It was true. Through her life, God had been speaking to people. That night, for the first time, she realised it. Her sickness was bringing glory to her Saviour.

Some months later she gave her testimony in a church in Cardiff. A lady slipped in at the back. She had come vowing this would be her last time in a church unless God spoke to her. A close friend had only that day been diagnosed with inoperable cancer; her husband had died years before in an IRA bomb explosion. She sat in the pew, desperate, feeling that God had deserted her.

Then Emma started to speak.

The pastor rang Emma later that evening. The woman had just left his home. She had asked God to speak to her and he had – through Emma. He just wanted her to know.

Emma put down the phone and cried. She sensed God's hand on her almost physically. He had come to her again and shown her unmistakeably that her life was not a strange twist of fate but part of his grand design.

He was using her sufferings – frail, insignificant Emma Freeman – to bring people to himself.

# Epilogue

Today, as I write, Emma is twenty-four years old.

Her latest neurosurgeon sees her once a year. In December 1998, after a routine brain scan, he wrote to her, stating with surprise: 'the tumour is visibly smaller'. Although what that implied he could not say.

She sees another specialist annually for her arm. Attempts to control its intermittent shaking have had varying degrees of success. Lenses have been prescribed to alter the appearance of her blown pupil. Her double vision remains. In December 1999 a cosmetic operation was performed on her eye to straighten it and prevent the eyelid flickering. She sees a heart specialist because of an abnormal heartbeat that appeared in 2000. Another specialist has been prescribing treatments successfully to counteract the gradual thinning of her hair.

In 2002 she underwent surgery to remove a fibroid from her uterus. Out of curiosity she asked the surgeon: 'How big was it?'

Blissfully unaware, he replied, 'About the size of an orange . . .'!

Despite advances in research and treatment no one has any medical solution to the tumour residing quietly in her head.

In the meantime, Emma remains spiritually defiant. She is an active member of her church, praying, attending everything, helping in the crèche and Sunday school. She invites family and friends to gospel services, welcoming everyone into the church. She helps in the local primary school, reading with children in the classroom once a week. She has a self-contained living space, built on to the bungalow, and has grown in independence, taking trips to visit friends on her own, without parental help.

She continues to give her testimony wherever and whenever she is asked.

Her love for God is obvious. One aunt spoke of a telephone conversation she had with her after calling to say she would be visiting from the States. 'What would you like to do when I come?' she asked Emma.

After a few moments Emma replied: 'I'd really like to have a quiet time with you, Aunty Sue'.

At the Fellowship of Independent Evangelical Churches (FIEC) conference, Easter 2000, she met up finally with the woman who had inspired her out of consuming depression, Joni Eareckson Tada. Joni signed her book, her pen in her mouth.

'Hey, how are you doing? Can I ask you what's happened to you then, Emma?'

After hearing her story she asked: 'How do you feel about Jesus now?'

Emma paused. 'I love God more today than yesterday.'

Joni started up a song, her sonorous voice rising over the crowded marquee: 'Jesus is better than the day before.' They sat side by side as crowds pressed around, vaguely interested in the two women in metal wheelchairs.

Yet the old struggles remain. Emma battles with fatigue and headaches. She continues to feel on the outside looking in as friends work, marry and have children. And always there is the cold uncertainty of her future.

In church one morning she was listening to a sermon on the book of Joshua: 'Have I not commanded you? Be strong and courageous. Do not be terrified; do not be discouraged, for the Lord your God will be with you wherever you go.'[8] The minister then read a quotation:

> Donald Hubbard, pastor of Calvary Baptist Church in New York City, told of spending a very difficult week at a youth camp some years ago. The teenagers from his church were at that time very cool and hardened toward the Gospel. On the final night, they had a campfire where the idea was to toss a stick into the fire, symbolic of one's life and commitment to Christ. The evangelist spoke and the offer was made, and no one responded. There was a girl with a disability there who had been shunned by the group all week because she was so hard to talk to – not that the kids were mean to her, they simply ignored her. Finally, she stood and faced the group, looking at each one, and said, 'I don't know why God made me this way, but he can have all of me'.[9]

Emma sat, ingesting the words. It would always be like this. Her life was uncertain, full of questions, but all the time God would break in and speak to her – just like now.

'I don't know why he made me with this tumour. I don't know why I am so incapable physically. I don't know what the future holds. But I know this. He can have me. He can have all of me.'

---

[8]  Joshua 1:9.
[9]  R. Kent Hughes, *1001 Great Stories and Quotes* (Illinois: Tyndale, 1998), p. 64.

*Emma meets Joni.*

*Fully involved in Sunday school.*